A STUDENT'S GUIDE TO
MUSIC HISTORY

THE PRESTON A. WELLS JR.
GUIDES TO THE MAJOR DISCIPLINES

Editor
Jed Donahue

༄

PHILOSOPHY   *Ralph M. McInerny*

LITERATURE   *R. V. Young*

LIBERAL LEARNING   *James V. Schall, S.J.*

THE STUDY OF HISTORY   *John Lukacs*

THE CORE CURRICULUM   *Mark C. Henrie*

U.S. HISTORY   *Wilfred M. McClay*

ECONOMICS   *Paul Heyne*

POLITICAL PHILOSOPHY   *Harvey C. Mansfield*

PSYCHOLOGY   *Daniel N. Robinson*

CLASSICS   *Bruce S. Thornton*

AMERICAN POLITICAL THOUGHT   *George W. Carey*

RELIGIOUS STUDIES   *D. G. Hart*

THE STUDY OF LAW   *Gerard V. Bradley*

NATURAL SCIENCE   *Stephen M. Barr*

MUSIC HISTORY   *R. J. Stove*

A Student's Guide to Music History

R. J. STOVE

WILMINGTON, DELAWARE

10/29/10

A Student's Guide to Music History is made possible by grants from the Lee and Ramona Bass Foundation, the Huston Foundation, Barre Seid Foundation, and the Wilbur Foundation. The Intercollegiate Studies Institute gratefully acknowledges their support.

Stove, R. J. (Robert James), 1961–

    A student's guide to music history / R. J. Stove.—1st ed.—
    Wilmington, Del.: ISI Books, c2008.

        p. ; cm.
        (Preston A. Wells Jr. guides to the major disciplines)
        ISBN: 978-1-933859-41-5

      1. Music—History and criticism—Outlines, syllabi, etc.
        I. Title. II. Title: Music history. III. Series.

ML161 .S76 2008   2007938117
780/.9—dc22   0801

ISI Books
3901 Centerville Road
Wilmington, DE 19807
www.isibooks.org

Design by Sam Torode
Manufactured in the United States of America

CONTENTS

৵

To my dear nephews,
Jimmy and Hugh

"History is the essence of innumerable biographies."

—Thomas Carlyle (1795–1881)

"One intellectual excitement has been denied to me. Men wiser and more learned than I have discerned in history a plot, a rhythm, a predetermined pattern. These harmonies are concealed from me."

—H. A. L. Fisher (1865–1940)

PREFACE

꒰꒱

A s the early Christian apologist Tertullian might
have said, this volume exists because it is impossible. The brief from ISI Books: to supply a student guide
to Western classical music's history, a guide that would
avoid both orgiastic one-upmanship and insults to the
adult intelligence; moreover, to keep this guide within
the word limits of its ISI series companions. The re-
sponse of almost any sane author to having been offered
this brief: pleasure and terror indissolubly combined.

Perhaps only P. J. O'Rourke, with his sublime knack
for discarding whole millennia of human history in a
sentence or two ("Man developed in Africa. He has not
continued to do so there"),[1] could manage such a reduc-
tive task to his own liking. Lowlier scribes find that the
deeper they go into the project, the sharper their panic
grows. By one means alone can they prevent fear from
incapacitating them: through seeking to make their
inadequacies work in their favor. For any twenty-first-

---

1. P. J. O'Rourke, *Republican Party Reptile* (London, 1987), 3.

I

century guide, tourism analogies are relevant. A package tour satisfies to the precise extent that it admits to being a package tour and does not pretend to be a pilgrimage or year-long sabbatical. When such satisfaction occurs, travelers may well find themselves rushed, but they cannot complain of being deceived. (Berkeley-based musicologist Richard Taruskin required six volumes and 4,252 pages for his 2005 *Oxford History of Western Music*. He still had to economize on various topics, particularly since he devoted two entire volumes to the twentieth century.)

The present book's resemblances to a package tour—a well-organized one, let us hope—will be obvious. Word limits enforce not simply depth limits, but range limits. What follows is necessarily, and therefore defiantly, Eurocentric. Where it ventures outside Europe at all, it mainly sticks to the United States. The whole phenomenon of artistic postcolonialism has inevitably been sidelined. So, still more unfortunately, has most nonclassical music: for space reasons, rather than through any latter-day desire for high-cultural gatekeeping.

Yet why (it might be asked) have a history, however brief, of classical music in the first place? After all, millions of sincere music-lovers derive genuine pleasure from their listening without any historical consciousness whatsoever. Australian discographer John L. Holmes observed in 1982: "A vast number of concert-goers have, I am amazed to find, an extraordinary ignorance . . . even of the common facts of musical history, and are puzzled why Bartók should sound so different from Haydn."[2] Writing in 1934, a far more overt pessimist, British composer-conductor-critic Constant Lambert, castigated "those to whom musical experience is no more than a mere aural tickling."[3]

Possibly within Lambert's pungent phrase lies the best answer to the question of why anyone should bother with music history. "Aural tickling," by definition, is evanescent in the pleasure it furnishes. A certain historical awareness gives, as it were, a three-dimensional effect to what one hears. It imparts the element of the composer's individual humanity; it banishes the assumption that the music concerned is a mere exercise in pattern-making. This is not a plea for biographical voyeurism, after the manner of tabloid hacks.[4] It is merely a plea for the life of the whole mind, for an end to the spiritual short-changing that comes from doing without historical knowledge in musical matters: or, worse still, from an active hostility to historical knowledge.

One innate problem afflicts any musical chronicle. No one historian can muster the same affection for every composer whom he describes. Frequently he finds

---

2. John L. Holmes, *Conductors on Record* (London, 1982), xii.

3. Constant Lambert, *Music Ho! A Study of Music in Decline* (London, 1934), 205.

4. Cf. Norman Lebrecht's "Why Conductors Have Great Sex" (*La Scena Musicale,* April 17, 2002), "Sex, Drugs, and Symphony Orchestras" (*La Scena Musicale,* June 22, 2005), and the rest of his book and magazine output, *passim.*

himself endorsing Oscar Wilde's dictum: "only an auctioneer can equally and impartially admire all schools of art." Readers of the following will discover that, now and then, the present author's judgment on a specific recent creator defies today's consensus. They are merely asked to believe that musical posterity is a bitch-goddess, repeatedly damning even the most honored composers of a particular epoch. A hundred and fifty years ago, such currently obscure figures as Giacomo Meyerbeer and Fromental Halévy stood unchallenged among composition's supreme immortals. During the same period, Johann Nepomuk Hummel and Louis Spohr were widely thought to surpass Beethoven. It is presumptuous to suppose that certain highly touted individuals of more modern times (particularly if their fame rests primarily on agitprop of nonmusical origins) will be any more impervious than were Meyerbeer, Halévy, Hummel, and Spohr to the turns of Fortune's wheel.

Inspiring genuine regret is the material that must be skimped. A chronological cut-off point has been, reluctantly, imposed. The coverage concentrates on those musicians who achieved at least national fame before 1945, with a brief epilogue essaying the futile task of summarizing post-1945 developments. When gripped by remorse over those deserving composers who have had to be slighted—or, too often, omitted altogether—one is tempted to embark on another book, simply to give these individuals adequate room. Meanwhile, the appended bibliography should help in furnishing information kept, perforce, out of the text proper. May it, and the guide it-self, lead to a renewed kindling of enthusiasm by readers for the subject: because any writing on music which fails to generate musical enthusiasm is done in vain.

> Music is a holy art,
> To unite all kinds of courage
> Like cherubs around a shining throne.
> —Richard Strauss, *Ariadne auf Naxos*

R. J. Stove
Melbourne, Australia
July 2007

FROM THE BEGINNINGS TO 1600

❧

HILDEGARD OF BINGEN, a German nun, poet, mystic, and advisor to princes, achieved international musical repute in the 1980s: no mean feat, since she had died in 1179. She is, indeed, the earliest composer whose output survives in bulk (around eighty pieces bear her name) and is regularly performed. "A feather on the breath of God," she called herself. If you heard her output without knowing what it was, you would probably take it for **plainchant** with instrumental accompaniment. Her works are, like plainchant, monophonic: comprising, in other words, a single melodic line. The instruments' contributions are mere editorial addenda.

Like every musician of her age and hundreds of years after, she lived and breathed plainchant. Pious belief credited Pope Gregory the Great, during the late sixth century, with having had this chant dictated to him by the Holy Spirit in the form of a dove. Alas, scholars now ascribe the chant—which continues to be widely and rather misleadingly known as "Gregorian"—to the time of Charlemagne, crowned Holy Roman Emperor in the year 800. Before acquiring this title, Charlemagne had imported papally approved chant to France, where it became intermixed with chant in native varieties before making its way across Europe, with Charlemagne's active championship. It eventually triumphed over other, formerly flourishing localized forms of chant: Mozarabic (native to Spain), Gallican (the original French form), and to a lesser degree Ambrosian (named after Milan's Saint Ambrose).

If Hildegard is for all practical purposes the earliest surviving composer, plainchant is for all practical purposes the earliest surviving musical repertoire. A few musical snippets—decipherable only conjecturally—from ancient Greece have endured to our day; of music from imperial Rome, not even that much. The "fiddle" with which Nero proverbially amused himself while Rome burned was, in reality, a lyre; what he played, we have no way of determining, just as we have no way of determining what King David played on his harp.

Such is the terrible fragility of musical knowledge from the days before globally standardized notation, let alone before sound recording. Musical notation first achieved a recognizably modern form at the hands of Guido d'Arezzo, a Benedictine monk (from Arezzo, Italy, hence his name) who around 1030 popularized staves on which to indicate musical pitches. Nothing like this had been systematically done in Europe before, and it required contact with Europe before other civilizations, however high, managed it at all.

Not that European notation achieved that much specificity itself until comparatively recent times. The familiar five-line stave is a thirteenth-century invention. For hundreds of years before that, a four-line stave was standard practice (in the reprinting of plainchant, it still is). It took till 1536 for music history's first tempo indication—in a Spanish collection of lute pieces, as it happens—to appear. Before the twelfth century the great bulk of all music remained monophonic. Continuous and consistent harmonization came only in the late twelfth century, with Paris's Notre Dame school, established just as Hildegard embarked on her old age. Who the specific European genius was who first managed to harmonize a given melody, we shall never know. (The likeliest guess is that originally such harmonizing was improvised rather than written down.) But that the Notre Dame school went further than any predecessors in codifying such harmonizations is beyond dispute. **Organum**, these instances were collectively called, and had been called well before Notre Dame. Léonin—or Leoninus, to use the Latin form of his name—is the Notre Dame school's earliest individual. He and his somewhat younger contemporary Pérotin (analogously Latinized as Perotinus) were hailed by a mysterious English student at Notre Dame, identified simply through the title "Anonymous IV," as "the two best composers of organum." By the time "Anonymous IV" wrote his tribute, both Léonin and Pérotin had long since died. They nevertheless continued to be esteemed long after their deaths, and no wonder. Most previous attempts at harmonizing had been extremely cautious, with the musical lines being frog-marched along to exactly the same rhythmic pattern. Léonin and Pérotin, on the other hand, positively exulted in soaring, rhythmically varied melodies that bore little relation to the sustained chords beneath them (if any), or to each other.

The Notre Dame school's pioneering efforts attest to how completely religion dominated medieval music. As well as attracting much of the best musical talent, the church preserved musical manuscripts better than did any other institution. Not solely manuscripts of sacred material, either: the irreverent, often lascivious thirteenth-century ditties whose words Carl Orff ransacked, during the 1930s, for *Carmina Burana* had been stored in a Bavarian monastery. By contrast, the Middle Ages' secular music largely lacks Notre Dame–style harmonic inventiveness. Like Hildegard's work, it is mostly monophonic. Again like her work, it carries no hints regarding instrumentation, which must be decided by modern editors. And it is intensely regional. The troubadours belonged mostly to Provence, though formal and stylistic elements of their aristocratic love songs found their way to northern France, where its practitioners called themselves *trouvères*. German-speaking territories responded to both troubadours and *trouvères* with their own courtly secular musicians, the *Minnesänger*. Yet despite the cross-fertilizing that sometimes occurred between these groups, what strikes today's observer is how tied to their original habitats they were: writing in their vernacular tongues, appealing to their own royal and noble courts' audiences, cramming their texts with political allusions mainly lost on later ages or foreign cultures.

With France's poet-composer Guillaume de Machaut (1300?–1377), there appears for the first time a figure who brought to secular composition the consistent dedication and ingenuity that had so long marked the sacred. Much admired by Chaucer for his amatory lyrics, Machaut left approximately four hundred verses behind him; he also gave the world its first non-plainchant Mass setting by a single hand, namely, the *Messe de Nostre Dame,* written around 1360 for Reims Cathedral. *Ars nova,* "New Art," is the name given even in Machaut's own time for the polyphonic elaboration and sheer rhythmic complexity of his (and certain of his contemporaries') idiom.

❧

AFTER MACHAUT, THE contest between sacred and secular for musical significance remained less hopelessly uneven than theretofore. Most composers for the next two hundred years served God and mammon with ease, although their ultimate allegiance stayed with God. Deriving with remarkable frequency from the Low Countries, they were peripatetic in a way that neither Machaut nor most of his secular precursors had been. John Dunstable (1380?–1453), an Englishman admired for his gifts in astronomy and medicine as well as music, spent time and owned land in France. His plentiful use of melliflu-

third-based harmonies—*la contenance angloise,* "the English countenance," as foreigners called this manner—formed a conspicuous contrast with Machaut's much edgier, more astringent, fourth- and fifth-based harmonic lexicon; and Continental musicians, during the early to mid-1400s, could not get enough of it. Those whom it influenced included Guillaume Dufay (1400?–1474), bastard son of a priest. Dufay spent years at Cambrai in northern France, but he also lived in Switzerland and Italy, alternating between ecclesiastical and noble employment. The somewhat younger Johannes Ockeghem (1410?–97) resided by turns in France and in what is now Belgium, sometimes visiting Spain and elsewhere; he cultivated fantastically elaborate counterpoint, sang bass, and wore glasses.

Similar cosmopolitanism, similar straddling of the sacred-secular divide, typified the generation born around the 1450 mark: notably Heinrich Isaac (1450?–1517), Josquin Desprez (1450?–1521), and Jacob Obrecht (1457?–1505). Isaac—known to Italians as *Arrigo il Tedesco*, "Harry the German"—spent his career at Innsbruck, Ferrara, and Florence. Obrecht, from Ghent, died in Ferrara during a plague outbreak. Josquin, generally viewed as the greatest composer of his time (Luther said of him, "He is master of the notes: others are mastered by them"), worked at Ferrara, Milan, Rome, and Paris. Once France's Louis XII, who combined love of music with almost complete incapacity for making it, asked Josquin to write a piece in which he could participate. Undeterred by the problem of royal talentlessness, Josquin confined the king's role to the singing of one repeated note, a reproof that Louis accepted with good grace.

This anecdote indicates the considerable freedom composers enjoyed under conditions often routinely denounced as "feudal." When a composer tired of his court or church post, he could and did abandon it with an alacrity that compels surprise. Some eminent musicians —Josquin for one —attained a reputation for arrogance. In no cases did such a reputation leave them permanently jobless. Netherlander Roland de Lassus (1532–94) acquired, when still in his early twenties, one of Rome's most prestigious musical directorships; within a year he had given it up, but far from suffering thereby, he achieved comparable heights in Munich, acquiring a papal knighthood. His two thousand extant works, all vocal, range from the loftiest Eastertide **motets** to the raunchiest drinking songs. Melancholia crippled his last decade.

ॐ

IN MANY RESPECTS Lassus constituted a reversion to medieval concepts of good clean dirty fun punctuated by austere piety, or vice versa. Lassus spent his life as if Protestantism had never happened. Not so the slightly older Palestrina, bound up in his career with a newly militant Catholicism, and accordingly on the defensive in a fashion that earlier church music-masters (*maestri di cappella,* as the collective Italian phrase has it) of similar fame had not needed to be. Far from bringing polyphony to new levels of elaboration, Palestrina purged it and clarified it. To pass from, say, a Mass setting by Ockeghem to one by Palestrina is to feel that, as it were, the incense has dissipated; that the words are much more readily audible; that the liturgical expression, however polished, is communal, as Ockeghem's sublimely introverted stratagems could never be. Like many great composers Palestrina represented an end, not a beginning. He predeceased Lassus by only four months, and with both men's departure there comes to the historian a sense that they had squeezed their respective styles dry. Younger men who tried to take after Palestrina (several had been his pupils) seldom produced more than wan imitations.

PALESTRINA, GIOVANNI PIERLUIGI DA (Italian, 1525?–94). Composer-laureate to the Catholic Church during the Counter-Reformation—admittedly, careless legend from long afterwards exaggerated his role as "savior of church music"—and acknowledged as the epitome of contrapuntal composition, although he saw himself as a practical artisan with a daily grind, rather than as a role model. He led a mostly quiet and uneventful life as music-master at various Roman churches, refusing lucrative job offers elsewhere. Extremely prolific, he wrote over a hundred settings of the Mass, and almost two hundred motets, along with a handful of (largely forgotten) **madrigals**. For all his devout compositional eloquence, he retained a level business head, periodically complaining if he thought publishers and paymasters were doing him down; in his fifties he married a rich widow. The honors that popes and cardinals showered on him he appears to have regarded as no more than his due. His best-known piece is the *Missa Papae Marcelli,* named after a short-lived pontiff (Marcellus II); other outstanding compositions from his

Already during Palestrina's lifetime his musical opposite had emerged: Carlo Gesualdo, Italian prince, as stylistically hyperemotional as Palestrina was superbly poised. In 1590 (his thirtieth year), Gesualdo had surprised his wife in bed with her lover and stabbed both of them to death. Untouched by official justice, he endured punishment of a subtler kind, insisting that his servants repeatedly and ritualistically flog him. As composer, in his madrigals and religious works he sought out ever more baffling harmonic progressions to express an anguish that he could never shake off. He died in 1613, possibly at his second spouse's hands.

❧❧❧

---

pen are the *Stabat Mater,* the *Missa Assumpta est Maria,* the *Missa Aeterna Christi Munera*, and the exultant motet *Tu es Petrus*. Apart from Lassus, his notable contemporaries included Tomás Luis de Victoria (1548?–1611), from Spain, and William Byrd (1540?–1623), from England. The former openly admired him, unlike the latter, who operated independently of Palestrina's influence.

FROM THE GABRIELIS AND MONTEVERDI
TO BACH AND HANDEL

❧

BY 1600, EUROPE's religious complexion had already become largely what it was to remain for centuries. Even the hideous carnage of the Thirty Years' War (1618–48) did not fundamentally change it. Before and after that war, various Protestant denominations prevailed in England, Wales, Scotland, Scandinavia, Holland (then called the United Provinces), northern Germany, and much of Switzerland; Catholicism prevailed in France, Italy, Spain, Portugal, Belgium (then called the Spanish Netherlands), Austria, southern Germany, and Poland. Consequently, outstanding musicians no longer crisscrossed Europe with the casualness they had displayed a hundred years earlier. Patriotism, musical and otherwise, now signified a good deal; for the likes of Dufay and Josquin, it had been meaningless. When English musicians, for example, sojourned abroad, they did so because they had to. John Dowland (1563–1626), exquisite master of the lute song, had disgraced himself at Elizabeth I's court by becoming a secret (but not secret enough) Catholic. The Catholicism of John Bull (1562–1628), more robust master of keyboard music, was overt and, in Elizabethan England, dangerous: hence his self-imposed exile, aggravated in his case by a record for purely secular crimes like housebreaking. William Byrd stayed at home, practicing his Catholicism in private while contributing in public—as his master and friend Thomas Tallis (1505?–85) had done—to the Anglican Church's musical settings.

More and more, particular states and city-states produced their own distinctive musical wares. Holland had Jan Pieterszoon Sweelinck (1562–1621), internationally renowned Amsterdam organist, pedagogue, and composer for his instrument. Rome tempered the severe ecclesiastical syntax of Palestrina and his school with that individual fancy which historians would come to call **baroque**. In the seventeenth century Rome's two best-known musicians were Girolamo Frescobaldi (1583–1643), who allegedly attracted thirty thousand hearers to his first organ recital, and Giacomo Carissimi (1605–74), notable principally for his short and didactic **oratorios** to Old Testament texts.

Venice shone in two different categories: it produced both Europe's most flamboyant church music and, afterwards, opera. The main Venetian church, Saint Mark's Basilica, housed the *cori spezzati* style. *Cori spezzati* means "separate choirs," and Venetian composers loved to pit widely spaced ensembles (both vocal and instrumental) against each other, rejoicing in the stereophonic—sometimes quadraphonic—results. Andrea Gabrieli (1510?–86) and his even more gifted nephew Giovanni Gabrieli

(1557–1612) brought this mode to its peak, amazing visitors with their music's sensual richness. An English tourist named Thomas Coryat wrote, in 1608, of *cori spezzati* music-making that it was "so superexcellent, that it did ravish and stupifie all those strangers that never heard the like." From Venice, the manner spread: Giovanni Gabrieli's pupils included Heinrich Schütz (1585–1672), who became the greatest of pre-Bach German composers and who said of his teacher: "Gabrieli, immortal gods, what a man!" Schütz's own output combined Gabrielian opulence with Teutonic solidity; his career, devoted largely to producing and directing Dresden's sacred music, lasted until he died at the age of eighty-seven.

The domination by Schütz of German music had its Italian parallel—after the younger Gabrieli's death in 1612—with the unchallenged supremacy of Monteverdi.

MONTEVERDI, CLAUDIO (Italian, 1567–1643). Proof that good things come to those who wait: in his case, who wait for almost three centuries in the grave. Having been the glory and marvel of music during his lifetime, especially his last three decades in Venice (previously he had been *maestro di cappella* in Mantua), Monteverdi fell after his death into a remarkable oblivion. During the eighteenth and nineteenth centuries his music slumbered unheard, and not till the 1930s did it start being performed again. Three operas by him survive: *Orfeo* (1607), *Il Ritorno di Ulisse in Patria* (1641), and *L'Incoronazione di Poppea* (1642). A fourth, *Arianna,* is lost save for one extract: the title character's lament "Lasciatemi morire," which drew tears from its original audience. *Orfeo*'s overture ("Toccata," Monteverdi called it) is among the most obviously gripping passages of music ever written, still awesome in its simplicity of means—little more than a decorated, repeated tonic major chord—and its effective-

His achievement and the early development of opera are inseparable from one another.

Before he arose, opera had been a fragile invention indeed. The Florentine Camerata, a late sixteenth-century group of aristocratic connoisseurs, sought to recapture the music of ancient Greek tragedy and realized that for this purpose old-style Palestrinian counterpoint was not a viable medium. Emphasizing monody (solo song with chordal accompaniment, often supplied by a lute), the Camerata sponsored the first surviving opera in 1600: *Euridice*, by one Jacopo Peri (1561–1633), to words by his colleague Ottavio Rinuccini. (Peri's music for an earlier collaboration between the two men is now lost, as is the first German opera, Schütz's *Dafne*.) The difference between *Euridice* and Monteverdi's first opera *Orfeo* is the difference between timid conscientiousness and magnificent panache. Monteverdi never allowed his audiences

---

ness of ends. As *maestro di cappella* at Saint Mark's Basilica, he maintained his commitments there throughout his operatic work, and at the age of sixty-five (by then a widower) he took holy orders. His *Vespers* of 1610 occupies perhaps an even higher artistic level than do the operas, which they resemble in tone. Also worth noting: his madrigals, of which he published eight books, running the emotional gamut from conventional nymphs-and-shepherds pastoralism to almost Gesualdo-like agony. The first composer known to have called for string tremolos, he admitted to being a self-conscious innovator. He argued in print that the "crudities" which fault-finders condemned in his music were entirely deliberate and should not be judged by existing criteria of polyphonic compositions, though in fact he could (and did) turn out such compositions with perfect fluency.

to forget that they were in a theater. Inserting abundant dances and choruses, he dispensed with Peri's cautious, often dull musical narrative and heightened the subject's innate expressiveness. His work recaptures the sheer ebullience of previous musical drama: such liturgical productions from the Middle Ages as *The Play of Herod* and *The Play of Daniel* (these Monteverdi never himself knew), along with the homiletic musical plays staged in his own lifetime by the Jesuits as aids to devotion (these Monteverdi may well have known). Within thirty years ordinary music-lovers were paying good money to hear the results. The first commercial opera house opened its doors in Monteverdi's Venice during 1637; Monteverdi wrote his two last operas, *Il Ritorno di Ulisse in Patria* and *L'Incoronazione di Poppea,* for commercial stagings.

Once Monteverdi had died, his operatic mantle fell on another Venetian: Francesco Cavalli (1602–76), who left thirty-odd operas, redolent of Monteverdi in their unabashed verve, but with a repeated melodic sweetness that looks forward to England's Henry Purcell. Cavalli, like most of his contemporaries (Schütz included), lavishly used the figured bass, alias ***basso continuo***.

Yet what Venetians loved, others resented, as Cavalli himself humblingly discovered in later life. When Cardinal Mazarin, France's de facto prime minister, commissioned from Cavalli an opera to celebrate the marriage of "Sun King" Louis XIV, the outcome was thoroughly sabotaged by local pride: in particular by a Florentine expatriate, Giovanni Battista Lulli, whose eventful résumé as kitchen-hand, violinist, dancer, and obscene versifier had made him more French than the French, and who had renamed himself Jean-Baptiste Lully. The ballet sequences that Lully (1632–87) devised for insertion into Cavalli's work achieved so much more popularity than the original that Cavalli fled Paris in disgust. After this triumph, Lully never looked back, despite the periodic scandals that his pederastic affairs caused. An absolute musical tyrant, he directed the French court's string orchestra— *Les Twenty-Four Violons du Roi*—with such discipline as to make it internationally honored. He exercised similar autocratic control over French theatrical music, doing his Machiavellian best to prevent such rival stage composers as Marc-Antoine Charpentier (1645?–1704) from being heard at all. (Charpentier stuck mainly, during Lully's lifetime, to religious compositions. From his *Te Deum in D* comes the world-famous Prelude, a favorite at weddings and employed by the European Broadcasting Union since the 1950s as its signature tune.) Finally, Lully's conducting proved, literally, the death of him. While directing his own *Te Deum* to give public thanks for Louis XIV's recent return to health, he kept time—as French custom then dictated—by regularly banging the floor with a staff. One such blow landed not on the floor but on his foot, and when the injury became infected, he succumbed to the consequent blood-poisoning.

Unlike Monteverdi and Cavalli, Lully continued to be revered after his death. So revered, in fact, that the chief French composer of the next generation, François

Couperin (1668–1733), avoided even trying to compete with him in the theater. Couperin, leading member of a musical family—hence his nickname, *Le Grand*—concentrated on harpsichord miniatures, where he showed genius. He revealed how much intensity can be crammed into the most delicate, artificial, courtly, precious of styles. Paradoxically, the greater Couperin's blue-blooded and periwigged elegance, the more widespread the sense of desolation behind it. His keyboard oeuvre is a masked ball that repeatedly threatens to turn into the Masque of the Red Death. Something of Couperin's mastery as miniaturist characterizes the harpsichord music of Jean-Philippe Rameau (1683–1764), but Rameau attained his greatest heights as Lully's theatrical successor. To his operas and opera-ballets (*Castor et Pollux, Hippolyte et Aricie,* and *Les Indes Galantes* are three of the most famous), Rameau brought a keener orchestral sense than Lully, a much greater melodic gift, and a superb cognizance of the French language's rhythmic nuances.

❦

THE SUN KING's control—exercised by judicious bribery—over Charles II across the Channel had its counterpart in France's influence over England's music. French banishment had given Charles a lifelong taste for French composition, and once restored to England's throne he wanted his court musicians to imitate and emulate it. This they did; but their works never wholly lost the tang of English soil. Henry Purcell (1659–95), very much the ablest of them, looked to Lully for specific musical effects. Nevertheless, the requirements of setting English differ so much from those of setting French that he could never have slavishly copied Lully even if he had wanted to. As Rameau perfected French vocal writing, so Purcell perfected English: not only in his sole conventional opera, *Dido and Aeneas,* but in more heterogeneous theater pieces such as *King Arthur* and *The Fairy Queen.* Purcell's great tragedy was twofold: first, his shockingly early death, probably from tuberculosis (though there long persisted a rumor that he succumbed to a chill caused by being locked out of his home while drunk by his wife); second, the umbilical connection between much of his music and the now unrevivable plays that it accompanied. There is no evidence that Purcell, an effortless melodist par excellence, deplored this wastage of his abilities.

Among musical history's greatest enigmas is the question of how Purcell, if granted a halfway decent lifespan, would have reacted to the arrival in England of Handel.

HANDEL, GEORGE FRIDERIC (German-English, 1685–1759). As cosmopolitan by temperament as Bach was German, Handel (who shared the year of his birth with Bach, and who will therefore be compared to Bach till the end of time) traveled widely on the Continent before making his eventual home in England. Regrettably, the oft-told tale that he wrote the *Water Music* in order to ingratiate himself with his old boss the Elector of Hanover, now raised to the dignity of King George I, has been disproven. Yet he habitually associated with sovereigns (from Queen Anne to the future George III) on more or less equal terms, made fortunes and spent them like an

During early youth, Handel had worked at Hamburg and various Italian cities. Everywhere he had been saluted, but only after moving permanently to London in 1712 did he accomplish recognition as one of the giants. He brushed aside competition from local composers as if they had been pygmies (by his standards, most were). Not literary himself, he nevertheless had too keen an eye

---

eighteenth-century Donald Trump, and generally did everything in his power to oppose the notion of a composer as a lackey whose place in life was below the salt. Wholly authentic is another anecdote of his early years: enraged with his colleague Johann Mattheson during a performance of one of the latter's operas, he fought a duel with him. "Luckily" (the words are an eighteenth-century chronicler's), "the sword of Mattheson was broke against a metal button upon Handel's coat, which put an end to the combat." Handel may have suffered from bipolar disorder (he wrote *Messiah* in only three weeks, while at other times his writing gift shut down altogether through sheer exhaustion); in addition, and with less plausibility, he has been spoken of as a homosexual (no man or woman has ever been identified as having a physical relationship with him). For two centuries most of his fifty (Italian-language) operas lay gathering cobwebs, their eventual vindication occurring only in the late twentieth century. Conversely, several of his twenty-three oratorios —*Messiah* of course, but also *Judas Maccabeus, Saul,* and *Israel in Egypt* —have had continuous performance traditions since they originally appeared. While Handel never lost his Germanic accent, he could express himself in English with a touch of sarcasm: he explained the commercial failure of his *Theodora* (among the few Handel oratorios *not* to use Old Testament words) with the words, "The Jews will not come because it is a Christian story, and the ladies will not come because it is a virtuous one." Like Bach, he went blind; unlike Bach, whose blindness lasted only for months, Handel remained blind for his final seven years.

for public relations to underestimate the value of pamphleteering, on his behalf, by others. Or the importance of governmental favor: it was he, not a native-born Englishman, who (a year before taking British citizenship) received the commission to write the four great **anthems** for George II's 1727 coronation. When poet John Gay and his friend, the minor musician Christoph Pepusch, mocked Handel's operatic manner—among other, juicier targets—in *The Beggar's Opera* of 1728, it was almost as if they had blasphemed. (They even plagiarized, for satirical emphasis, Handel's own music.) Historians used to maintain that *The Beggar's Opera* capsized Handel's own operatic ventures, but in truth it amounted to a mere passing, if irritating, nuisance. Not until the late 1730s did Handel wind down his own opera production—which was making him broke—and concentrate on English-language oratorios, for which he occasionally recycled some of his operatic material. To musical performance he brought the smack of firm government, once upstaging his vituperative soprano Francesca Cuzzoni by grabbing her waist and threatening to defenestrate her. "You are a veritable she-devil," he roared, "but I would have you know that I am Beelzebub, the chief of devils." As if this hands-on leadership did not suffice, he would take the solo role in his own organ concertos, which he used as fillers for oratorio renditions. The English judged one final abode alone to be fitting for him: he now rests in Westminster Abbey.

❧

ON HIS EARLY Rome tour Handel had met Arcangelo Corelli (1653–1713), the most respected Italian musician of his time, who confessed to bewilderment at his visitor's eclecticism: "My dear Saxon [*mio caro Sassone*]," Corelli admitted, "this music is in the French style, of which I have no knowledge." Corelli, a professional violinist, shone in suavity; at his best he had something of Purcell's unforced inspiration, although without Purcell's drama, and much of Couperin's grace, although without Couperin's sorrowful undertone. Uniquely among Italian composers in his day, he avoided vocal music, confining himself to chamber works and ***concerti grossi,*** this last genre being most famously represented in his output by the posthumously published *Christmas Concerto.*

Through an odd caprice on Time's part, other Italian composers of Corelli's period have been remembered almost exclusively for their own instrumental writing, despite having thought of themselves primarily as operatic practitioners. The most spectacular victim of this gulf between intention and current fame is Antonio Vivaldi (1678–1741), who composed forty operas, all now unheard, except on the rare occasions when a latter-day star like Cecilia Bartoli records highlights from them. Known as "the Red Priest" (from the color of his hair), Vivaldi confined his sacerdotal duties to a minimum in order to concentrate on his employment as music-master at a Venetian orphanage, the Pietà. For the Pietà's own, all-female orchestra he produced most of the five hundred concertos that have kept his name alive. An old joke charges Vivaldi with composing "the same concerto five hundred times," but what might have passed muster as an authoritative assessment before World War II is untenable now that so great a proportion of Vivaldi's music has been resurrected. Occasional overuse of convenient harmonic formulae cannot obscure the overwhelming inventiveness elsewhere. To adorn *The Four Seasons*, Vivaldi actually wrote a set of four sonnets, thus displaying a poetic talent rare among composers of any age. Certainly his fellow Venetian Tomaso Albinoni (1671–1751) had no such authorial interests, being, indeed, a far more pliable and less highly strung character. Albinoni produced fifty operas, even more totally forgotten than the Red Priest's have been. It is hard luck that his name survives principally because of the spurious *Adagio*, which is actually a fantasia by a twentieth-century musicologist, Remo Giazotto, based loosely on a six-bar Albinoni fragment. At least the two compositions by Giovanni Battista Pergolesi (1710–36) that still enjoy frequent revival are their creator's unaided efforts: *La Serva Padrona*, a one-act operatic comedy that has retained a following when most Italian stage works from the period gather blankets of library dust; and the *Stabat Mater*, itself thoroughly operatic in style, which dates from the last year of Pergolesi's woefully short life.

La Serva Padrona belongs to the intermezzo genre, having been intended (as most such one-acters were) to provide comic relief for the serious piece that took up most of the evening. No one devoted himself with greater strenuousness to furnishing such serious pieces than Alessandro Scarlatti (1660–1725), active mainly in Rome and Naples, who produced more than one hundred operas in total (some, admittedly, light comedies). A pitifully small amount of his work endures in popular remembrance: half a dozen arias; a dozen orchestral items to be found in a few chamber ensembles' programs; the occasional Mass setting. Alessandro had the additional misfortune to father a composer more immediately appealing than himself: Domenico Scarlatti (1685–1757), a model to late-bloomers everywhere. Until his forties Domenico was just one more nondescript provider of music—mostly sacred, always forgettable—in Rome. In 1729 he went to Spain, becoming music teacher to the Portuguese-born Queen Maria Barbara, whom he had met years previously while visiting Lisbon. His Madrid residence and educative duties inspired his unparalleled series of 555 keyboard sonatas: mercurial, virtuosic, sometimes evoking Iberian folk dance, and (despite such evocations) spectacularly original. A myth that he grew fat in old age, and thus needed to dispense with the multiple hand-crossings his earlier sonatas required, does have a basis in fact: the obesity sufferer was not he, but Maria Barbara.

⁂

THE ABILITY TO ignore most contemporaries distinguished Scarlatti's muse; the ability to absorb, and then to surpass, most contemporaries distinguished Bach's. Having taken all musical knowledge for his province, Bach—heir of a musical dynasty, like Couperin—measured himself ceaselessly against composers living and dead. As a child

---

BACH, JOHANN SEBASTIAN (German, 1685–1750). "The most stupendous miracle in all music," Wagner called him. There are dozens of clichés about Bach, all of them, to varying extents, justified: the baroque's quintessence and summation, the most ingenious contrapuntist of all, the most complete natural genius music has ever produced, the supreme musical theologian, the supreme musical mathematician, etc. And, on one occasion, a breathtaking liar: "Work as hard as I do," he once advised a pupil, "and you will do as well as I do." Born in the same year as Handel and Domenico Scarlatti, Bach never met either man, though he knew of both and particularly admired the former. (The peripatetic Handel was out of town when Bach had hopes of meeting him.) One critic wrote that "Bach was an organist widened out, and Handel an opera-manager deepened"; this comparison, for all its inadequacy, may be as good a description as any other of the two complementary geniuses' respective personalities. Bach's contemporaries considered his creativity a side-issue to his performing (in addition to his choral direction, he mastered the violin and all the keyboard instruments of his time). It is typical that his official obituarist failed to mention his feats as composer. The frequency with which Bach bawled out, and occasionally brawled with, inept musicians under his charge can inspire only envious wonderment among twenty-first-century choirmasters. As hardheaded a working stiff as Palestrina, and still more prolific, Bach viewed himself less as an artist than as a vessel for divine use. His musical credo: "to the honor of God and the edification of my neighbor." *Soli Deo Gloria*, "To God Be the Glory," he often wrote at the end of a piece. For all the splendors of the *Saint Matthew Passion,* the *Saint John Passion,* the *Mass in B Minor,* the four *Orchestral Suites, The Well-Tempered Clavier* (the first masterpiece ever to use all twenty-four major and minor keys) and the six *Brandenburg Concerti,* no one can claim to know Bach who has not sought out

he studied, under his elder brother's tutelage, works by Frescobaldi, Lully, and Johann Pachelbel (1653–1706) of subsequent *Canon* fame. As a youth he walked two hundred miles to hear the great organist Dietrich Buxtehude (1637–1707) play. As a mature man he repeatedly returned to his copies of scores by Vivaldi and Albinoni, among others, often rearranging these pieces for his own use, and usually improving them in the process. Technique, technique, technique: that obsession, rather than any archeological interest, fueled Bach's seemingly endless appetite for examining and internalizing other composers' achievements. It is as if his only moments of unalloyed happiness occurred at his desk. Indubitably, such moments were few enough in his workaday directorial practice. In 1717, a blazing row with his boss at Weimar led to his being jailed for almost a month. The best he could say of the fifty-four boy choristers under his care at Saint Thomas's School in Leipzig—where, from 1723 till his death, he labored as cantor—was that "seventeen are competent, twenty not yet competent, and seventeen incapable." His Leipzig paymasters, in what remains one

---

his sacred cantatas—approximately two hundred of them survive, another hundred having been lost—and his organ works. There Bach stands (or rather kneels), working out his salvation "in fear and trembling," as Saint Paul urged. Poignant biographical nuggets: of his twenty offspring, eleven died in childhood; and after losing his sight late in life, he is said to have been (uselessly) operated on by the same English doctor who treated, with equal lack of success, Handel.

of music's most notorious misjudgments, resigned themselves to hiring Bach merely because they could not obtain the services of his middlebrow rival, Georg Philipp Telemann (1681–1767), probably the most fecund composer who ever lived. (Telemann—a good friend of Bach's—produced, inter alia, forty-four Passion settings; twelve sets of sacred **cantatas**, with fifty-two pieces in each set; forty operas; and six hundred overtures. He himself lost count of what he had written.) Eventually, Bach, so far as the Leipzig job would let him, reduced his performing commitments, concentrating upon writing the instrumental masterpieces of his last years: above all, *A Musical Offering* and *The Art of Fugue*, where his contrapuntal prowess reached peaks even he had not always scaled before. The latter work makes prominent use of the punning four-note theme: B-A-C-H (in German, "B" stands for B flat, "H" for B natural). Amid its nineteenth section, the manuscript abruptly breaks off after the B-A-C-H motif appears one last time. Before Bach could finish it, he died.

2&2&2&

FROM GLUCK AND BACH'S SONS
TO BEETHOVEN AND SCHUBERT

৵৻

Pity Bach's sons. Confronted with the perfection of their father's accumulated utterance, they would have been superhuman not to have resented it, not to have thought his influence oppressively old-fashioned. (Less pardonable is their description of him as "the old *perruque* [powdered wig]," and their failure to prevent his widow Anna Magdalena from dying in want.) Of these sons, the eldest, Wilhelm Friedemann Bach (1710–84), was the old man's favorite and may have had the greatest natural ability. This he soon dissipated in a career remarkable above all for the ease with which he lost many of his father's manuscripts and his propensity for wandering off whatever jobs he obtained. Carl Philipp Emmanuel Bach (1714–88), a more formidable figure, went in stylistic directions that even the most recondite of Johann Sebastian's ventures never suggested. The German literary movement known as *Sturm und Drang* (roughly, "Storm and Stress") coincided with C. P. E.'s activity, and he provided its musical equivalent with his sometimes

freakish harmonic progressions, his melodic patterns'
huge jumps hither and yon, and his taste for dramatic
pauses. The overall effect is of a hot-tempered improvisation. He took over Telemann's old post at Hamburg,
having previously been keyboard player at Frederick the
Great's Prussian court, where his sharp tongue found little sympathy in Frederick's circle. (After one somewhat
incoherent performance by Frederick on the flute, with
C. P. E. accompanying him, a courtier gushed: "What
rhythm!" C. P. E. muttered: "What rhythms!") With
Johann Christian Bach (1735–82), alias "The London
Bach" because of his protracted English residence, all is
sunny elegance. J. C.'s output, which musicologists usually describe by that convenient if untranslatable term
galant, has far more in common with the late eighteenth
century than with anything in his father's production.

Equally uninterested in Johann Sebastian's manner
were the musicians of the Mannheim School. Their lead-
er, violinist and conductor Johann Stamitz (1717–57),
instilled in Mannheim's orchestra a discipline unrivaled
anywhere in Europe. Touring English historian Charles
Burney called this brilliant ensemble "an army of gener-
als." To display it, Stamitz himself wrote around fifty
symphonies and thirty concertos. He stressed—as did
other Mannheim composers—such attention-grabbing
techniques as the "Mannheim Rocket" (broken chords
leaping up from the lowest instruments to the highest),
and the "Mannheim Crescendo" (an ever-increasing
number of instruments). Like Lully, Stamitz mattered

more as drillmaster and stylistic systematizer than as composer. Today he and his colleagues are recalled less for their own attainments than for their writing's influence on Haydn.

———————

HAYDN, JOSEPH (Austrian, 1732–1809). Was there ever, among composers, a more total contrast between image and reality than Haydn's case supplies? Millions *think* they know him: "Papa Haydn" (this patronizing description surely being a deterrent in itself), neat, liveried, garrulous, vaguely recollected as "the Father of the Symphony," and, to be candid, rather boring. This was not the Haydn whom music-lovers of his own time prized: the only eighteenth-century composer whose sheet music was gobbled up as far afield as Lisbon and Saint Petersburg. (Unscrupulous publishers airily attached the name "Haydn" to numerous inferior efforts by other men, since anything thus identified would abundantly sell.) For three decades Haydn worked as music director at the palace of the (Hungarian) Princes Esterházy, exhibiting, as befitted a servant, flawless courtesy combined with fundamental toughness. On the Esterházys' staff, to quote his own words, "I was cut off from the world, there was no one to confuse or torment me, and I was forced to become original." His 104 canonical symphonies have a much lower dross quotient than even Mozart's forty-one, and the last twelve in particular—written not for the Esterházys but for the London-based impresario Johann Salomon—are among the form's outright masterworks. Although a few others wrote string quartets before Haydn, no predecessor had endowed the medium with the drama, humor, and balance among voices that Haydn commanded. *The Creation* is among the few oratorios that survive comparison with Handel's and Bach's. His Mass settings, while utterly disregarding Palestrinian criteria for dignified sacred composition, are often triumphantly successful as concert music in church. In the field of the piano trio he is unchallenged. His wife (he married her on the rebound from her sister) earned herself an unenviable immortality by using her husband's manuscripts to line her pastry tins and curl her hair.

Lasting longer in its impact than the Mannheimers' virtuosity was the operatic reform of Vienna-based Christoph Willibald von Gluck (1714–87). Gluck had one thing in common with Domenico Scarlatti a generation earlier: his gifts developed exceptionally late. Between his twenties and his late forties he ground out some thirty operas (some in Italian, some in French), none of which attracted more than passing notice. Then, in 1762, he suddenly erupted into the first rank of operatic masters with his *Orfeo ed Euridice*. With this, he and his collaborator, poet Ranieri de' Calzabigi, arrived at a lofty directness, a mostly syllabic kind of word-setting, an often richly accompanied **recitative,** and an end to the excessive vocal acrobatics of too much previous operatic fare (though Gluck admired Handel's). In the published preface to *Alceste*, five years later, Gluck emphasized his message afresh: "I have striven to restrict music to its true office of serving poetry by means of expression and by following the situations of the story, without interrupting the action or stifling it with a useless superfluity of ornaments." His subsequent operas lived up to this aim. They included *Paride ed Elena* (1770), *Iphigénie en Aulide* (1774), and *Iphigénie en Tauride* (1779), the two last-named composed for Paris. He had been appointed Queen Marie-Antoinette's singing teacher, and with this royal backing he directed his operatic performances with a dictatorial rigor far surpassing even Stamitz's approach. His later music greatly impressed various French-domiciled opera composers, such as André Grétry (1741–1813).

❧

NOT THAT GLUCK held a monopoly on operatic procedures at the time. Earlier, less severe, less reformist styles
continued to exist. For instance, Haydn, although seldom thought of as an opera composer at all, did write
two dozen operas—mainly for his Esterházy employ-
ers—including five for marionettes. Those occasionally
revived in our time have been for the most part genially
florid, un-Gluck-like pieces. Although they elicited much
admiration in the composer's own day (Austrian Em-
press Maria Theresa once announced "If I want a good
opera, I go to Esterháza" [the Esterházy estate]"), they
were swiftly forgotten afterwards. Closer to Gluck's lega-
cy were certain operas of the young Mozart. The latter's
Idomeneo (1781), especially, has much Gluckian grandeur
in it, though Mozart had little time for Gluck personally
and envied the older man's financial success.

MOZART, WOLFGANG (Austrian, 1756–91). No, not "Amadeus"; his
baptismal certificate reads "Joannes Chrysostomus Wolfgangus
Theophilus Mozart," "Amadé" (the form of his middle name that
Mozart himself preferred to use) being Theophilus's Gallicized version. In fact, almost everything else Hollywood told you about him
is wrong, except his child prodigy status, which even Hollywood
could hardly have invented. The face that launched a thousand
chocolate boxes belonged to one who seethed with anger over rivals now largely forgotten; whose repeated failures to obtain or keep
well-paid jobs with emperors and prelates derived in almost every
case from his own inability to hold his tongue; and who employed
servants even during his worst periods of Viennese impoverishment,
a detail irksome to sentimentalists. One thing in his largely misbe-

Haydn managed more permanent distinction with the genres of the symphony and the string quartet. These run through his creative life like two golden threads. Even the earliest Haydn symphonies, with obvious hints of Stamitz's school, have a subtlety and variety for which nothing at Mannheim prepares the listener. They indicate Haydn's irrepressible *joie de vivre*, which his fairly wretched upbringing as choirboy (he and his fellow trebles seem never to have been adequately fed) could have overwhelmed but somehow left intact. Although never a face-to-face pupil of C. P. E.

---

gotten career he did get right: he acknowledged Haydn's genius, and a symbiotic relationship existed between the two men. To a minor composer who sniffed at an unconventional passage of Haydn's—"*I would not have written it that way*"—Mozart delivered a bruising snub: "Nor would I. And do you know why? Because neither I nor you would have thought of it!" Difficult though it is to single out a solitary area of Mozart's chamber composition for special applause, his string quintets are almost universally regarded as excelling all else that he produced in chamber genres. Of Mozart's mature operas, *The Marriage of Figaro, The Magic Flute,* and *Don Giovanni* have been favorites for most of the last two centuries. *Così Fan Tutte,* on the other hand, only entered the repertoire after World War II, its few stagings before that date having often been in bowdlerized versions. No aspiring pianist would even consider ignoring the best of Mozart's twenty-seven concertos; similarly, no aspiring conductor could possibly ignore Mozart's three last symphonies, including the *Jupiter.* The list goes on. There are 626 items in the official catalogue of Mozart's works, a catalogue compiled not by Mozart but by nineteenth-century musicologist Ludwig Köchel (hence the "K" that appears before the number of a particular composition). When it comes to discovering Mozart, you have your whole life before you.

Bach, Haydn studied C. P. E.'s music thoroughly and most respectfully. His own contribution to the *Sturm und Drang* ethos is detectable in several symphonies he wrote during the 1770s, though even here he avoided C. P. E.'s more eccentric gambits. After 1780 his symphonic style broadened and stabilized, becoming more majestic, as his *Paris* and (later) *London Symphonies* testify.

Concerning the string quartets, overall trends are harder to discern. Haydn tended to write them in bunches, rather than with the consistent dedication he brought to producing symphonies. The earlier quartets are at times so atypical that it was unsurprising when, in the 1960s, several of them turned out to be by another musician. In his Opus 33 quartets of 1781—written, as he himself said, "in an entirely new and special way"—Haydn first showed greatness with the medium. This greatness he confirmed through such later achievements as the *Emperor Quartet* (so called because it includes a set of variations on Haydn's own *Emperor's Hymn*) and the so-called *Razor Quartet* ("I would give my best quartet for a good razor," Haydn assured a visiting English publisher, who supplied the razor and was given the rights to a new quartet in return). At this juncture honorable mention should be made of the composer's younger brother Michael Haydn (1737–1806), a man of talent, as opposed to Joseph's genius, but demonstrating enough worth—especially in sacred music—to suggest that posterity would have treated him with greater esteem if his surname had been different.

The elder Haydn, with his earthy realism and sane self-confidence, happily praised his best rivals. He famously assured Mozart's father, Leopold: "Before God and as an honest man, I tell you that your son is the greatest composer known to me, either personally or by reputation." Sometimes Haydn and Mozart performed quartets together, their colleagues being two lesser but still significant musicians, Karl Ditters von Dittersdorf (1739–99) and Johann Vanhal (1739–1813). Leopold's diligence at exhibiting his child-prodigy son in numerous cities (including Munich, Frankfurt, Cologne, Vienna, Brussels, London, Paris, Rome, Naples, and Milan) is still celebrated, and his wisdom still questioned. On one side of the ledger is the psychic damage Mozart incurred as a boy because of so unrelentingly itinerant an existence. On the other side, and less often noted, is the fact that almost all eighteenth-century childhoods were, by modern standards, horrible; moreover, it remains unclear whether hiding a child prodigy's light under a bushel serves that prodigy any better in adult life than does publicizing his gifts. Indisputable is the tortured nature of the father-son relationship once the son became an adult: Leopold dutiful, unimaginative, canny, fearful of social slights; Wolfgang headstrong, supremely imaginative, improvident, blisteringly contemptuous of most others' opinions.

Never of Haydn's opinion, though: he cherished Haydn as Haydn cherished him, and the power of Haydn's mature quartets inspired him to write better music (not only chamber music) than he had ever previously done. Nearly all Mozart's outright masterpieces date from his last decade, when a new polyphonic richness entered his writing, derived partly from studying Haydn's work and partly from Bach's and Handel's scores. Mozart often appeared indifferent, during his later years, as to whether he had commissions or not. "Genius does what it must," the saying runs, "and talent does what it can." His three final, and most glorious, symphonics were all composed (in 1788) without prospects of performance; he seems never to have heard them, a sobering fact when one recalls how accessible they are in the early twenty-first century. It is hardly credible that the two operas from his last year on earth should have been from the same hand: *La Clemenza di Tito*, statuesque, neo-Gluckian, an acquired taste; and *The Magic Flute*, that resplendent hotchpotch of fairyland, freemasonry, pantomime, and poetics, an unending delight to the connoisseur, while also being infinitely lovable by all children aged nine to ninety-nine.

Among the few European regions Mozart never visited was Spain, where dwelt a curiously isolated figure: Luigi Boccherini (1743–1805), who operated independently of Mozart's influence, as the younger Scarlatti had operated independently of Bach's and Handel's. Boccherini—eminent cellist as well as composer—incurred the scornful posthumous description "Haydn's wife." The more of Boccherini's output is rediscovered, the less convincing this tag becomes. Traces of Scarlatti junior, instead, characterize his manner, which tends to greater playfulness, and hedonistic charm, than Haydn and Mozart even at their most jocose. He concentrated on chamber works, notably more than one hundred string quintets and approximately ninety string quartets.

❧

HAYDN, WHEN PLANNING his second (1794) visit to London, seriously considered bringing with him a pupil of his from Bonn (Germany), only twenty-three years old, but already exhibiting greatness: Beethoven. Originally

---

BEETHOVEN, LUDWIG VAN (German-Austrian, 1770–1827). The words credited to Mozart after a Beethoven performance—"Watch that young man: he will make a great noise in the world"—read like something out of a fourth-rate movie director's vapid imagination, but they actually seem to be authentic. Beethoven's whole career may be said to have alternated between the wildly improbable and the merely impossible. The deafness, for a start: far from being spiritually destroyed by it, he gave us his most inspired creations only after he lost his hearing. (He confined the destruction to the pianos that had the misfortune to be played by him: strings would pop out, hammers fall off.) His sketchbooks contain more abundant, and higher, inventions than many another composer's finished products; moreover, the very fact that they were considered worth keeping is in itself an indication of how Romanticism laid increased emphasis upon the artist-hero. However musically abstruse he grew, he never lacked admirers, though he also never lacked detractors. Confining ourselves to a mere handful of Beethoven's 135 opus numbers, we behold: nine symphonies, of which the odd-numbered ones (notably the *Eroica,* the Fifth, the Seventh, and the choral Ninth) have been consistently more cherished than the even-numbered; thirty-two piano sonatas, ranging from the daintiest urbanity to (especially in

Beethoven had hoped to study with Mozart, and among the tragedies of Mozart's early death is the way it prevented this particular sustained meeting of minds. Yet perhaps Beethoven, like Mozart, derived more from his self-imposed study than he could ever have done from formal instruction, even Haydn's. In youth he became Vienna's greatest pianist since Mozart's demise. His earliest published compositions appeared in 1795, and he quickly revealed much greater skill than Mozart at finding rich aristocratic patrons to subsidize his creativity. Not for Beethoven the dependence on a circumscribed palatial job. Fortunately for his quest, he possessed considerable personal allure. While not conventionally captivating—he never learned to dance, his face bore pockmarks, and his swarthy complexion gave him the soubriquet "the Spaniard"—he had a circle of devoted music-loving friends. He seemed unstoppable.

Destiny decided otherwise. Sometime in 1796 he noticed a constant ringing in his ears. At first, and with great adroitness, he concealed his auditory problems from others. Eventually the tinnitus drowned out all else. Conversation became impossible. He played on out-

---

the *Hammerklavier*) the most implacable majesty; the *Missa Solemnis*, shattering and at times almost unsingable; the seventeen string quartets, of which the last six are at once the most bewildering and the most powerful; the opera *Fidelio*, which he revised twice and for which he supplied no fewer than four overtures; and the *Kreutzer Sonata* for violin and piano, which famously haunted Tolstoy. And this list does not even include the second division of Beethoven's output.

of-tune pianos without realizing their pitch problems. Doctor after doctor, miracle cure after miracle cure: all availed nothing. No mere paraphrase can match the 1802 letter that he himself wrote, but never sent, to his brothers (known as the *Heiligenstadt Testament*) when contemplating suicide. It reads, in part:

> "Oh, you men who think or say that I am malevolent, stubborn, or misanthropic, how greatly do you wrong me. . . . [I]t was impossible for me to say to people, 'Speak louder, shout, for I am deaf.' Ah, how could I possibly admit an infirmity in the one sense which ought to be more perfect in me than others?"

Four years later we find him noting, on the manuscript of his three *Razumovsky Quartets* (thus called because Count Razumovsky, Russian ambassador to Austria, had commissioned them): "Let your deafness be no longer a secret—not even in art." A singularly pregnant remark, this, at odds with eighteenth-century concepts of artistic decorum. So is Beethoven's famous outburst at the news of Napoleon's coronation as emperor. Having dedicated his *Eroica Symphony* to the Corsican general, he furiously crossed out the name "Bonaparte" from the title page (which still exists). Impossible to imagine Bach, Handel, or even Mozart thereby openly defying any ruler, however tyrannical.

Ever greater isolation from the world, ever richer music: such is the tale of Beethoven's concluding years. An anguished, proto-Dickensian legal case over the custody of his nephew; a pitiable scene during the Napoleonic conquest of Vienna, where he frantically squeezed pillows over his head to shut out the din of bombardment (like so many people in deafness's early stages, he had excruciating sensitivity to unwanted noise); and, as if possessed by a hundred demons, the frenzied composing. All his greatest string quartets and piano sonatas, his *Missa Solemnis,* the last six of his symphonies—these all appeared after his career as a pianist had ended. After 1818 he no longer understood speech even if the speaker (as a fellow composer commented) shouted loudly enough to be heard three rooms distant. His ear-trumpets did him no good; he could communicate only by writing.

In his last illness, he examined some manuscripts that a young man had finally nerved himself to send. "Truly," Beethoven said of these pieces' composer, "he has the divine spark." The young man was Schubert.

SCHUBERT, FRANZ (PETER) (Austrian, 1797–1828). As has been repeatedly pointed out, if everything of Schubert's except his songs were to disappear, the best songs would still guarantee him a place with the greats. For all his devotion to Beethoven, he contrived, paradoxically, to stay as little influenced by Beethoven's style as any impressionable Viennese artist could be. His tireless fertility of invention rendered useless the standard analytic verbiage about Austro-German music's "first subjects," "second subjects," and "bridge passages." More positively, it moved Robert Schumann—a great admirer—to speak of Schubert's "heavenly length," this phrase having become a cliché for subsequent musicologists, particularly when they deal with the *String Quintet in C,* the piano sonatas, and the *Wanderer* piano fantasy. Any list, however brief, of Schubert's fin-

All his adult life, Schubert worshipped Beethoven. Now, a gesture of kind recognition from Olympus. What might this gesture have done for Schubert had it come earlier? Would it have given him enough self-respect to make him quit his habitual hand-to-mouth bohemianism? None can say. Quiet, plump little Schubert—his friends called him *Schwammerl,* meaning "little mushroom" or, figuratively, "tubby"—remains mystifying, as several much more deliberately cryptic composers do not. Suspected of revolutionary and freethinking sentiments, Schubert nevertheless stayed, at least formally, within the Catholic Church in which he had been nurtured. He composed as naturally as he breathed. Whereas Beethoven slaved over every phrase as if sawing through granite, Schubert routinely discarded entire symphonies and operas with less regret than most of us feel at abandoning extracted teeth. Why? That answer also eludes us. During his final months he contemplated undertaking the most rigorous possible course in contrapuntal composition; would this course, if attempted,

---

est songs—his entire song output is now available on CD—would need to include *The Erlking, Gretchen at the Spinning Wheel,* and two song-cycles of his last years: *Die Schöne Müllerin* and *Winterreise.* The reasons, incidentally, for his *Unfinished Symphony* remaining unfinished are mysterious. Recent assertions that Schubert was actively homosexual may or may not be accurate. He undeniably contracted syphilis, though he seems to have been killed by either typhus or typhoid. Once he sent some of his most impressive songs to Goethe, who did not even bother to acknowledge their arrival.

have deepened his art (surely deep enough already?) or cramped it? Again, no answer.

What we do know is that Schubert viewed Beethoven's genius as something forever unattainable; as "the immortal beloved," it might be said, remembering the name that history applies to the great love of Beethoven's life, a love whose identity is still uncertain. At Beethoven's funeral, Schubert—literally—carried a torch. Late the following year Schubert himself came to rest, as he had hoped he would, in a grave next to Beethoven's own. The epitaph provided for his tombstone by his fellow Austrian, poet Franz Grillparzer, remains unsurpassed: "Music has here interred a rich treasure, but still fairer hopes."

⁊⪤⪤⪤

FROM WEBER AND ROSSINI
TO WAGNER AND VERDI

❧

"THE OLD ORDER changeth, yielding place to new." These words are from 1845 (a Tennyson poem), but the sentiment they express had started affecting musicians decades earlier. Emblematic of the new Romanticism was Carl Maria von Weber (1786–1826), born eleven years before Schubert, yet appearing to represent a much younger generation. Weber embodied all the Romantic spirit's trends. Early death (note his dates); personal recklessness (he ruined his voice by drinking engraving acid); patriotism; lifelong preoccupations with folklore, with the forest (that most conspicuous feature of the German Romantic landscape), with the Middle Ages' chivalry, with ghosts and devils, with Things That Go Bump In The Night. And, perhaps above all, a commitment to literary explanation. This was especially novel. Bach, Handel, Haydn, Mozart, even Beethoven, would have found a manifesto-writing urge incomprehensible. Weber, on the other hand, spent almost as much time writing *about* music as writing it. Among his musical works, the greatest is his 1821 opera *Der Freischütz*, which proclaimed his absolute mastery of the macabre and which so successfully set down German roots that several of its tunes have attained the status of folk songs. Later operas, *Euryanthe* and *Oberon,* have lovely things in them but have never held the stage.

If Weber was German Romanticism's father, his French counterpart was Hector Berlioz (1803–69), also a copious—though in his case bitterly reluctant—journalist. Unable to live off his own music, loud in his distaste for the Paris Conservatoire instruction he had undergone, and incapable of playing an instrument in public, Berlioz had a brilliant prose style through which he lauded Gluck, Mozart, Beethoven, and Weber, all unfamiliar to most Frenchmen at the time. (His enthusiasms stopped well short of Handel, whom he dismissed as "a tub of pork and beer." He also unjustly ridiculed the Conservatoire's distinguished director Luigi Cherubini [1760–1842], whose output Beethoven had praised.) Of Berlioz's 140-odd compositions, the most renowned is his *Symphonie Fantastique* (1830), characteristically subtitled "Episodes in the Life of an Artist": a five-movement, stunningly orchestrated extravaganza motivated by his infatuation for Irish actress Harriet Smithson, whom he later, disastrously, married. Later pieces include *Harold in Italy* (1834), based on Byron's *Childe Harold*; a monstrous and stirring *Requiem* (1837), whose performing forces famously require four brass bands; *The Damnation of Faust* (1846), a "dramatic legend" occupying disputed territory between oratorio and the theater; and *Les Troyens,* a noble operatic treatment of Virgil (spread over two evenings) considered too unmanageable for complete performance during his lifetime or, indeed, till 1890. Scandalizing foes and sometimes friends by the sheer awkward originality of his inspirations, Berlioz observed to a well-wisher: "Yes, given another 130 years I might see a career opening out ahead of me."

Harold had been commissioned by the greatest violinist of the time and, maybe, of any time: Niccolò Paganini (1782–1840), whose histrionic, superstar virtuosity—gossip credited him with having sold his soul to, or alternatively with being fathered by, Satan—constituted the nineteenth-century musical equivalent of bungee-jumping. Alas for Berlioz, Paganini rejected the finished *Harold* as being not nearly spectacular enough. But Paganini did at least as well without Berlioz's music as he would have done with it. Tall and cadaverous, he had the advantage of looking like the freak that he was. Pianists as well as his fellow violinists stood in awe of him. By his public persona, as much as or more than by his own (often superficial) composing, he enlarged the concept of what musicians thought technically possible.

After Paganini, practically every musician not yet a virtuoso wanted to be one. Robert Schumann (1810–56) suffered especially from this desire. In his labors to become a great pianist, he permanently damaged his right hand. Thereafter he concentrated on his own creativity, through words as well as through notes: he wrote abundant, often sharp criticism for his own Leipzig-based magazine, *Neue Zeitschrift für Musik*. His earliest mature musical works were piano solos: *Papillons, Carnaval, Scenes from Childhood*, and *Fantasy in C,* among others. Having thus proved to be one of the most gloriously fanciful purveyors of a true pianistic language, he married (1840) Clara Wieck, daughter of his former piano teacher and herself a pianist of rare talents. Overflowing with love, he poured out his heart in songs, of which he wrote 168 in his first year of wedded life. Many of his songs match Schubert's in standard. Though he rarely had a light touch in his orchestration, his four symphonies and three concertos (piano, violin, and cello) contain much irreplaceable poetic charm. But the tragedy of his frustrated pianistic ambitions foreshadowed the much greater tragedy of his mental breakdown. Always prone to panic and auditory disturbance, he found it ever harder to cope. In 1854 he tried to drown himself, and he spent his remaining years in an asylum at Bonn.

During his healthy days, Schumann had fought the good fight via the *Neue Zeitschrift*. His judgments, sometimes harsh, were never craven. "The laws of morality are also those of art," he announced. With his fellow contributors, whom he called the *Davidsbündler* ("League of David")—because they so fiercely opposed the era's Philistines—he reprehended the cheap and the crass: "One who refuses to attack the bad is but a half-hearted supporter of the good." His targets included Giacomo Meyerbeer (1791–1864), who had become the rage of Paris with his grandiose operas, including *Robert le Diable, Les Huguenots,* and *Le Prophète.* "Fit only for a circus," Schumann snapped. About Meyerbeer's rival Gioacchino Rossini (1792–1868), Schumann could be equally brisk: "To the multitude it is, of course, a matter of indifference whether Beethoven wrote four overtures to a single opera [*Fidelio*] or whether Rossini equipped four operas with a single overture." (Rossini possessed an incorrigible habit of recycling his own material. The overture to his comic masterpiece, *The Barber of Seville,* had already served for two previous stage efforts.)

Schumann had little more enthusiasm for Rossini's fellow operatic Italians, Gaetano Donizetti (1797–1848) and Vincenzo Bellini (1801–35), though the most notable achievements of all three composers deserve worthier remembrance than Schumann himself believed. These men represented the manner known as **bel canto** (though that actual phrase dates only from around 1850). Donizetti, responsible for creating eighty-odd operas within twenty-nine years, necessarily perpetrated much forgettable hackwork; but three of those operas—*Lucia di Lammermoor, Don Pasquale* and *L'Elisir d'Amore*—are permanent parts of the standard repertoire, while others, such as *La Fille du Régiment* and *Lucrezia Borgia,* occasionally reappear to good effect. When informed that Rossini had finished an opera within a fortnight, Donizetti good-naturedly commented: "He always was a lazy chap." Almost unbelievably, Donizetti finished *L'Elisir d'Amore* within a week of receiving the **libretto;** his inspiration bears no hint of haste. (A caricature of the time depicts him as composing simultaneously a comic opera with one hand and a tragic opera with the other.) As for Bellini, he had a greater delicacy of musical feeling than either of his seniors, a much more measured output rate, and an aptitude for creating slow melodies that seem to stretch forth, like grand straight Roman highways, to a far distant horizon, notably "*Casta diva*," the best-known aria from his best-known opera *Norma*. Other tolerably familiar Bellini operas are *La Sonnambula* and *I Puritani*. "Opera, through singing," he once said, "must make one weep, shudder, die"; Donizetti and Rossini never spoke thus. A devotee of Pergolesi, Bellini declared himself willing to make do with a similarly short lifespan and in fact succumbed to dysentery—a most inappropriate fate for so aristocratically refined an artist—when not yet thirty-four.

⁊⋲

BELLINI'S ADMIRERS INCLUDED Frédéric Chopin (1810–49), who, in turn, had been ecstatically greeted in a Schumann essay: "Hats off, gentlemen, a genius!" Warsaw (where Chopin underwent his early musical schooling) lay far enough from the European artistic mainstream to give Chopin exotic appeal, as of a distinctive and lasting scent. His own Polish pride burst forth only after he had left his homeland for good, assisted into permanent exile by the failure of Poland's 1830–31 uprising against Russian domination. The oft-told story that he bore away with him a small packet of Polish soil, to be scattered over his grave when he died, is improbably maudlin but true. His reworkings of Polish dance forms—the polonaise and the mazurka especially—surpassed anything earlier composers had attempted. While they exploited these genres for splashes of local color, he channeled his inmost thoughts into such genres with the utmost naturalness.

Tubercular from early manhood, he seems in some respects the Romantic virtuoso's archetype. Only afterwards do the differences between Chopin and most of his colleagues clearly emerge. For example, he mostly avoided verbal explanations of his musical impulses. Except for his four *Ballades*, which have some connection—still much debated—to verses by his countryman Adam Mickiewicz, he eschewed nonmusical allusions in his output, preferring neutral titles: *Etudes, Nocturnes, Preludes, Sonatas, Waltzes,* and so forth. (He never coined such later nicknames as *Raindrop Prelude* and *Funeral March Sonata*.) Far from being the swashbuckler of popular imagination, he performed so delicately as to be almost inaudible in large halls. Probably his renditions seemed even softer than they were, given his superbly imaginative use of the piano's sustaining pedal and the extra sense of mystery this use generated. At times such introversion irked his mistress, the transvestite novelist, dramatist, and cigar-smoker Aurore Dudevant, who used the pen-name "George Sand" and who once snakily referred to Chopin's mother as "his only passion." Their relationship defied the odds by lasting nine years. She hoped that he would shake off his sickness in the dry climate of Majorca; he could not; a subsequent Scottish sojourn's rigors helped kill him. His best music, with considerable force beneath its witchery—Schumann well likened it to "flower-banks concealing guns"—endures wherever pianos are played. This despite its narrowness of medium: for almost every meritorious thing Chopin wrote is a piano solo (his two piano concertos and twenty songs rank well below his most significant inspirations).

While Chopin epitomized single-minded concentration, Felix Mendelssohn (1809–47) epitomized versatility, combined with a youthful brilliance beyond even Chopin's and Schumann's. Like Schumann but unlike Chopin, he came from a highly bookish environment. The philosopher Moses Mendelssohn had been his grandfather; he himself—baptized when still a child—hobnobbed on familiar terms with Goethe. Before his eighteenth birthday he had already produced three of his greatest works: the *Octet*, the overture to *A Midsummer Night's Dream* (the rest of his music for that play came much later), and the fantastically evocative concert overture *The Hebrides*. From a ludicrously early stage, he shone wherever he turned his hand: not only in most compositional genres, but in sketching, painting, pianism, organ-playing, and conducting. An untiring traveler, inveterate in his industry, and on occasion downright cruel—"Berlioz's instrumentation is so disgustingly filthy," he told his mother, "that one needs a wash after merely handling one of his scores"—he worshipped Bach. To him we owe the first posthumous performance (Berlin, 1829) of the *Saint Matthew Passion*. This performance inspired Mendelssohn to marvel in public at the music's neglect. Alluding to his thespian colleague Eduard Devrient as well as to himself, he remarked: "To think that it should be an actor and a Jew who have given back to the people the greatest Christian work."

If ever nineteenth-century music had a golden mean, Mendelssohn is it. Avoiding Chopin's ballroom glitter and Schumann's more literary exuberance, he created at least one masterpiece in almost every form. The *Violin Concerto* and *Italian Symphony* retain their initial freshness; his oratorio *Elijah* ranks not far below Handel; his *Songs Without Words* have worn far better than many other piano miniatures much more complex; his six organ sonatas are among the finest organ pieces written by anyone between 1750 and 1850; and though some of the most worthwhile songs published under his name were actually by his elder sister Fanny, the authentic songs from his pen are uniformly agreeable and often more. His tidy intellect abhorred ranting, fumbling, and undue repetition. In an 1842 letter he enunciated his crisp artistic credo: "The thoughts which are expressed to me by music that I love are not too indefinite to be put into words, but on the contrary, too definite."

THE PHRASE "TOO definite" could never have featured in any utterance by Franz Liszt (1811–86), who made his whole existence a veritable rampage of indefiniteness, of squaring the circle, of mystic aims and carnal appetites, of angelic concord and demoniacal wrath. He brought to the piano the same stupendous technical bravura that Paganini (whom he hugely honored) had brought to the violin. Carried away by his showmanship, women shrieked, fainted, and flung themselves at him. One besotted admirer kept in her undergarments, for twenty-five years, the butt of a cigar that the great man had smoked. A staggeringly gifted sight-reader, Liszt often grew bored with others' music after the first play-through and would add to it what Mendelssohn called "tomfool pranks. . . . I could have listened to many a middling pianist with more pleasure." Consciously echoing Louis XIV, Liszt proclaimed: "*Le concert, c'est moi.*" Performing for the much-dreaded Tsar Nicholas I, he stopped playing once Nicholas began to talk. "Pray continue, Monsieur Liszt," ordered the Tsar. "When Your Majesty speaks," replied the imperturbable Liszt, "all others should be silent." He intended for his own use the wild and flashy music he poured forth in youth. Most of it could have been called, as some of it actually was called, *Studies in Transcendental Execution.* Over a decade he gave more than a thousand concerts, astounding audiences from Dublin to Constantinople. In him, the medieval concept of the vagrant musician, with all Europe for his home, achieved a revival. Yet for all his imperious keyboard deportment, he repeatedly craved a life in which the nomadic virtuoso had no place, and in 1847 he gave up professional pianism forever.

Nevertheless, Liszt did not thereby achieve more complete musical integration. Of all world-famous composers he was surely the least consistent, alternating magnificent utterances with reams of catchpenny trash. His pre-1847 domestic life had been dominated by his affair with a French countess, Marie d'Agoult, which produced two daughters: Blandine (who married French Prime Minister Emile Ollivier) and Cosima (who will reappear in this text). Liszt's other great love—primarily during the 1850s—was a Polish princess, Carolyne Sayn-Wittgenstein, under whose firm didactic hand he attained prominence as conductor (notably at Weimar) and augmented compositional innovation. But though these middle years witnessed much of Liszt's most impressive music—including the *Faust* and *Dante* symphonies, the **symphonic poems** *Les Préludes* and *Orpheus*, and the *Piano Sonata in B Minor*—he always remained prone to banality. When he took minor priestly orders in 1865, he merely made an already tangled existence still more controversial, particularly since his clerical collar left unimpeded his womanizing. "Mephistopheles in *abbé's* garb," historian Ferdinand Gregorovius called him. A tireless piano teacher in Rome and Budapest as well as Weimar, he became—and is still—a Hungarian national hero, though he scarcely spoke the Hungarian language, and though his celebrated *Hungarian Rhapsodies* derive from gypsy music rather than from indigenous folklore.

His singular kindness to younger composers exacerbated his disinclination to promote his own best output. "I can wait; meanwhile, my shoulders are broad," he observed. Frequently his later pieces intensify his persistent harmonic venturesomeness, and sometimes (as in *Via Crucis* for choir and organ, or the appropriately named *Bagatelle Sans Tonalité* for piano) they abandon key-centers entirely. Yet they are seldom performed and exhibit a curious sense of struggle, as if their creator's theatrical tendencies could not be denied even in his most sincere vein.

If Liszt craved the limelight, his almost exact contemporary Charles-Valentin Alkan (1813–88)—whose pianistic skill survived comparison with Liszt's own—shunned not only the limelight but most human society. As obsessive as Liszt was discursive, Alkan specialized in producing hair-raisingly difficult piano studies, playable by hardly any other pianists in his time or until the 1960s. One of his better-known pieces is a funeral march for a parrot; Monty Python would have approved. From his thirties onward he seldom performed in public, concentrating instead on thoroughgoing study of his Jewish faith. The much-quoted tale that he was crushed to death by a falling bookcase (when trying to reach his copy of the Talmud) is apocryphal, but the truth is scarcely less strange: he apparently climbed up an umbrella-stand, fell, and died from the resulting injuries.

PARIS, SO GENEROUS a host city to Liszt, Alkan, and Chopin (as well as Rossini, Donizetti, Bellini, and Meyerbeer), proved inhospitable to a turbulent figure whose life would be lastingly connected with Liszt's: namely, Wagner. Like Berlioz, Wagner never played a musical instrument adequately; again like Berlioz, Wagner conducted a good deal. He shared Berlioz's voracious appetite for literature while lacking Berlioz's self-mockery and verbal panache. Where he differed from Berlioz above all was in yoking his own destiny to the opera house. From his early twenties, he tried to instill some musical discipline into a series of mostly ramshackle German operatic troupes, fortified in this task by little more than his prodigious determination, belief in himself, and—when he wanted to exercise it—charm.

WAGNER (WILHELM) RICHARD (German, 1813–83). One simple, amazing statistic says it all: more books have been written about Wagner than about anyone else in history except Christ and Napoleon. Wagner himself would have considered this verbiage to be no more than he deserved. "I am the German spirit," he once told his diary, immediately proceeding to discuss "the incomparable magic of my works." But as so often with Wagner, what seems like psychotic boasting proves, on closer inspection, more complicated. The "German spirit" he persistently hailed bore little relation to the Germany he saw with his own eyes. Exiled from German soil for over a decade, he ultimately found comfort and a worshipful following not among the northerners of whom he had once entertained such high hopes, but in Bavaria. This is almost the least of the paradoxes that mark Wagner's life. Among others: the extreme sangfroid by which, with no hope at the time of performance for *Der Ring des Nibelungen,* his magnum opus, he suddenly abandoned work on the

Refusing to have his wings clipped by an authorial collaborator, Wagner always wrote his own libretti. For his third opera, *Rienzi* (two earlier efforts misfired), he had the highest hopes; and these hopes included having it staged in Paris. There everything went wrong. *Rienzi*—overwhelmingly trite, by the standards of Wagner's most valuable compositions—much resembled the feasts of spectacle with which Meyerbeer consistently stunned crowds; but with the real Meyerbeer flourishing in their midst, Parisians felt little interest in an imitation Meyerbeer from abroad. Wagner resentfully eked out a liv-

---

cycle's third opera (*Siegfried*) to write *Tristan und Isolde* and *Die Meistersinger von Nürnberg,* so utterly different from one another and from *Siegfried* itself. *Tristan* constitutes an achingly lugubrious and ecstatic portrayal of doomed love, while *Die Meistersinger* reveals an almost Shakespearean sense of humane comedic compassion for ordinary folk. Within the *Ring* cycle—*Das Rheingold* and *Die Walküre* both preceding *Siegfried, Götterdämmerung* bringing the tetralogy to a close—lies an extraordinary range of moods. Very little in music is more terrifyingly thunderous than *Götterdämmerung's* climaxes, more delicate than *Siegfried's* "Forest Murmurs," or nobler than *Das Rheingold's* "Entry of the Gods into Valhalla." Wagner's plentiful use of *Leitmotiven* (literally "leading motives," or themes signifying individual characters, places, soul-states, and so on) served, both in the *Ring* and in his other great works, as connective musical tissue. Yet notwithstanding his passion for continuity, he has often been heard in the form of concert extracts (widely, if disrespectfully, known as "bleeding chunks"). Standing outside his operatic achievement, but thematically related to it, is Wagner's smallest masterwork: the *Siegfried Idyll,* an 1870 birthday gift to his second wife and scored for chamber forces.

ing with journalism and musical hackwork. At times he went hungry. On his return to Dresden, *Rienzi* enjoyed immense acclaim. Emboldened by such success, he produced two more operas, *The Flying Dutchman* and *Tannhäuser*, both of them overtaxing the musical resources at hand, and neither initially well received by hearers. At this point he had far outgrown *Rienzi*'s braying pomp. The "art work of the future"—his own phrase—that he imagined, and wanted to create, owed nothing to Meyerbeer and precious little to any Italian models (although he did respect Bellini). He wished it to be a quasi-religious rite in itself, much as the Greek tragedies that he had loved since boyhood served religious functions in their day.

During 1849, with Wagner's goal still a mere dream, Dresden erupted. Wagner sided with the revolutionary movement, proclaiming his own anarchism. When the revolution collapsed, he fled, pursued by Saxon police and (an equally grave menace) Saxon debt-collectors. Not Saxony alone, but the other German states were now closed to him. He spent twelve years in Switzerland, composing little at first, but pouring out essays, ranging from mostly preposterous spite (as with his diatribe *Judaism in Music*) to profound aesthetic commentary (as with *Opera and Drama,* where he expounded the concept of "endless melody" that would so dominate his own later music). Before escaping Dresden he had finished another opera, *Lohengrin*, and implored Liszt to have it produced. Liszt eagerly did so and further helped Wagner out by lending him money as well as by championing his music. Meanwhile, Wagner concentrated on devising a libretto derived from ancient Norse sagas and the anonymous twelfth-century *Nibelungenlied*. This libretto he initially intended to call *Siegfried's Death*; but its plot grew so elaborate that he found himself writing a prologue to clarify it, then another prologue to clarify the first prologue, and then another prologue to clarify the second prologue. When setting these libretti to music, however, he did so in chronological order. Twenty-eight years elapsed between his first sketches for the whole gigantic project, which became *Der Ring des Nibelungen*, and the last notes of the scoring.

This heroic exertion, alas, seemed incapable of bringing him any income. For all his sponging talents, he could not extract "loans" from friends perpetually. The ban on his German residence ended in 1861, but without noticeably improving his monetary condition. Two of his other operas, *Tristan und Isolde* and *Die Meistersinger von Nürnberg*, remained stubbornly unperformed. Only a lunatic could have predicted for him an altogether happy future. Fortunately there emerged just such a lunatic: Bavaria's King Ludwig II. Having adored Wagner's music ever since childhood, Ludwig lavished on the composer a villa, hard cash, and promises to stage Wagner's most recent operas. Some hiccups did occur. Ludwig insisted on having the *Ring*'s first two operas staged in Munich against Wagner's will. Moreover, Wagner took Liszt's daughter Cosima as his mistress, thereby cuckolding one of his most devoted advocates, the brilliant conductor Hans von Bülow. This alliance (the couple married in 1870) estranged both Wagner and Cosima from Liszt for several years. Finally, and nevertheless, all the mutual admiration between Wagner and King Ludwig bore spectacular fruit. Wagner obtained his own opera house at Bayreuth; and there, in 1876, the complete *Ring* cycle had its première. *Parsifal*, his last work—"a sacred festival drama," to quote his own description—was first given at Bayreuth six years later, only seven months before Wagner's death.

❧

WAGNER'S PROSE WORKS take up eight fat volumes and include discourses on almost every imaginable topic. Among the extremely few subjects that failed to interest him was his great and almost exact contemporary Verdi.

VERDI, GIUSEPPE (FORTUNINO FRANCESCO) (Italian, 1813–1901). "I am not a very learned composer but I am a very experienced one," wrote Verdi, ever the practical man of the theater. Sensitive about his lack of formal education (Milan's music college, to its everlasting disgrace, rejected him, partly because it considered him—at nineteen—"too old"), he rejected during his fifties the offer of a Naples professorship. This refusal sprang both from his distaste for urban ways and from his reluctance to appease colleagues in the manner that a music school would have forced on him. He could be downright bloodthirsty, as a remark he made during the struggles of 1848 reveals: "Do you think I want to concern myself now with notes and sounds? There should be only one kind of music pleasing to the ears of Italians of 1848—the music of the guns." Fortunately, this con-

Pages could be spent contrasting these two composers (who, like Bach and Handel, never met): Wagner the verbose German theorist, Verdi the blunt Italian pragmatist; Wagner the spendthrift, Verdi the frugal product of smallholding peasant stock near Parma in Italy's northwest; Wagner writing his own texts, Verdi repeatedly obliged to set whatever doggerel hack librettists offered him. Though the two men shared an absence of institutionalized musical schooling, this absence manifested itself in different ways: Wagner sneered at such schooling; Verdi (who could play the piano and organ) would have liked it, yet could not obtain it.

Verdi's third opera, *Nabucco* (1842), became his first international smash hit, not least for its great chorus of Hebrew slaves, "*Va, pensiero.*" *Nabucco* proved a personal, as well as a professional, milestone. Giuseppina

---

tempt for his own creativity soon passed, and he showed afterwards a capacity for sympathizing with figures whom he might have been expected to resent. Wagner, for instance, had called Verdi's *Manzoni Requiem* "a work of which it is better not to speak," but Verdi, on hearing of Wagner's demise, told his publisher Giulio Ricordi: "Sad, sad, sad, Wagner is dead!" A tireless combatant—opposed to this very publisher, if necessary—for proper royalties and against pirated editions of his own operas, Verdi never lost the bucolic shrewdness of his ancestors. This trait infuses his art with a fundamental sanity, to which his fellow Italians gratefully responded. But he schooled himself to be as indifferent as possible to others' cheers or jeers: "I accept its [the public's] whistles, on the condition that I am not asked to give back anything in exchange for its applause. For three *lire* the audience buys the right to whistle or applaud. Our destiny is to resign ourselves to the situation."

Strepponi, an erratic and fast-living soprano celebrated primarily for having wrecked her voice by her early thirties, temporarily overcame her executant handicaps and shone in the virtuoso part of Nabucco's daughter Abigaille. A few years later she became Verdi's mistress. This concubinage scandalized Verdi's neighbors and relatives, but his own religious skepticism left him impervious to local Catholics' snubs and threats of hellfire.

Meanwhile, pressures of work dominated everything. His creative schedule (like Donizetti's) would have killed a weaker man: thirteen operas between 1843 and 1851. Understandably, he described this period as his "galley-slave years." It was too much. Of these thirteen pieces, *Ernani, Macbeth,* and *Luisa Miller* stood out, *Macbeth* having met Shakespeare on something like his own terms; most of the remainder no more hinted at Verdi's subsequent merits than *Rienzi* hinted at Wagner's.

In *Rigoletto* (1851), contrariwise, Verdi achieved consistent greatness. And though censors fretted over its depictions of aristocratic debauchery, audiences loved it. In addition, they loved its successor, *Il Trovatore* (1853), with its notoriously convoluted storyline and its breathtaking melodic appeal that renders the convolutions irrelevant. They initially hated *La Traviata* (also 1853), based on a *roman à clef* that dealt with a recently deceased French courtesan, Marie Duplessis (whose lovers included Liszt). Nonetheless, after Verdi had lightly revised the score, *La Traviata*—attaining a sublime tenderness new to him—succeeded as spectacularly as it had once failed.

Between *La Traviata* and *Aïda* (first staged in 1871 at Cairo's new opera house), Verdi arrived at an increased profundity of feeling but sometimes appeared to lose his certainty of touch. *Simon Boccanegra, La Forza del Destino,* and *Don Carlos* all contain some of his most powerful music but are allied to confused texts. *Un Ballo in Maschera* (1859, the year that Verdi and Giuseppina became man and wife) brought censorship trouble once again. Alarmed by a theatrical reenactment of regicide—in this case, the 1792 murder of Sweden's Gustavus III—the censors demanded that the opera's locale be changed to colonial-era Massachusetts.

By the time that *Aïda* appeared, Verdi's Italy had become almost unrecognizably different, in political terms, from what it had been a generation earlier. Verdi himself had heartily approved of Italy's escape from Austrian governance and its gradual unification, at first under the aegis of Turin-based statesman Camillo Cavour. So much did Verdi esteem Cavour that, overcoming his aversion to most politicians, he actually served in the legislature from 1860 to 1865. For decades Verdi's operas had been widely interpreted as onslaughts against Austrian oppression and as propaganda favoring national control by Cavour's boss, Victor Emmanuel of Piedmont (eventually king of all Italy): the cry *"Viva Verdi!"* could be, and often was, interpreted as code for *"Viva Vittorio Emmanuele Re D'Italia!"*

After *Aïda*, many expected Verdi to retire gracefully. He did not. His *Manzoni Requiem*—written to honor the country's main nineteenth-century novelist, Alessandro Manzoni—flabbergasted those who assumed that he had no bent for religious music. Routinely called "an opera in ecclesiastical dress" or, more waggishly, "Verdi's best opera," it confirms his growing interest in piquant orchestration. In old age he turned to the literary flair of a much younger man, Arrigo Boito (1842–1918), who had known brief prominence as a composer with his opera *Mefistofele* but had acquired a separate reputation as librettist. Boito collaborated with Verdi on his two last and greatest operas, both Shakespearean in origin: *Otello* (1887) and *Falstaff* (1893). Verdi had never written anything as subtle, as luminous, as frequently exquisite, as these final masterpieces, the former a searing tragedy, the latter a moonstruck will-o'-the-wisp of a comedy. Both showed that his genius had expanded and deepened as his youthful fluency declined. When he died in Milan, it was as if a national monument had been ripped from Italy's terrain: two hundred thousand mourners beheld the funeral procession.

꒰ꕀ꒱꒰ꕀ꒱꒰ꕀ꒱

FROM BRAHMS AND BRUCKNER TO
SIBELIUS AND STRAVINSKY

ॐ

WITH BELLINI AND Donizetti dead, with Rossini
ensconced in princely retirement, Verdi had become by his fortieth birthday not only Italy's greatest active composer, but Italy's sole great active composer. He
continued to occupy this exalted position until, near the
end of his life, a new Italian school emerged. Of the two
figures who could have been Verdi's serious rivals, Boito
sank into musical desultoriness (his long-promised follow-up to *Mefistofele* remained unfinished), while Amil-
care Ponchielli (1834–86) had great operatic success with
La Gioconda—which Italian theaters still sometimes re-
vive—and was never heard from again. (Boito had written for Ponchielli *La Gioconda's* libretto, credited to "To-
bia Gorrio," an anagrammatic pseudonym.)

Wagner could not dominate Teutons' music-making
as totally as Verdi dominated Italians'. He had to share
leadership of German-speaking composers with three
contemporaries: Anton Bruckner (1824–96), Johann
Strauss Jr. (1825–99), and Brahms. A fourth, Max Bruch

(1838–1920), fell slightly below this level of eminence but honorably upheld the best traditions of secure Germanic workmanship with his large output, most of which—save for his ever-popular *First Violin Concerto*—has been entirely forgotten.

Brahms, solidly gifted from an early age both at the piano and in composing, inspired—when only fourteen years old—the following optimistic tribute from his teacher Eduard Marxsen: "A master is gone [Mendelssohn had just died]; a greater master arises in Brahms." Schumann, sick in body and in mind, rallied for long enough in 1853 to give Brahms's earliest pieces a rave review: "he has come, this chosen youth, over whose cradle the Graces and Heroes seem to have kept watch." Through the last agonies of Schumann's life, Brahms stayed faithfully at the family's side and regularly visited the hapless patient in his asylum. Clara Schumann outlived her husband by four decades. It seems that she would have happily married Brahms (fourteen years her junior) if only he had found the courage to ask her. In-

---

BRAHMS, JOHANNES (German, 1833–97). The popular instinct that equates Brahms with Bach and Beethoven as one of the "three Bs"—Hans von Bülow seems to have been the first person to lump those three composers together—has this to be said for it: of all great composers Brahms was the most historically aware, weighed down by his encyclopedic knowledge of ancient musicians as diverse as Schütz and Couperin. Hence his decision to delay writing any of his four symphonies until his forties: his first earned from Bülow the accolade "Beethoven's Tenth," a half-truthful description that nettled Brahms

stead, he and Clara maintained a rapturous but platonic friendship, much of it epistolary, until death. "Whatever you write," he once ordered a poet, "ask yourself if a woman like Clara Schumann would look upon it with approbation. If you have any doubts, cross it out."

Most of Brahms's juvenilia he afterwards destroyed. Simplicity of diction never came naturally to him, nor did creative effervescence. He grumbled: "You have no idea how it feels for someone like me to hear behind him the tramp of a giant like Beethoven." Nonetheless he retained enough stoicism to arm him against passing fail-

---

himself. Like Beethoven, Brahms combined bachelorhood with waspishness, though regrettably, he did not in fact utter the epigram attributed to him: "If there is anyone here whom I have not insulted, I beg his pardon." He hated empty virtuosity—during a Liszt recital he is said to have fallen fast asleep—but his piano compositions, in particular, abound in practical difficulties and failed to enter the mainstream repertoire until long after his death. His lifelong deep love of Bach and Handel emerged in, above all, his *German Requiem* (not a Requiem Mass setting, despite its name: Brahms, a Protestant insofar as he practiced any creed, simply set to music various verses from Luther's Bible). Bernard Shaw might have complained that this Requiem "is patiently borne only by the corpse"; posterity's verdict on it has been much more welcoming, and its place among the nineteenth century's finest choral works is now unassailable, as are the places of all his symphonies among the nineteenth century's finest orchestral works. In the field of song, Brahms can often stand alongside Schumann and Schubert. His chamber music is, on the whole, less performed and less attractive (an exception is his late and movingly nostalgic *Clarinet Quintet*). He lived long enough to make—in 1893—a sound recording, in which he plays the piano (badly) and utters a few words of greeting to Thomas Edison.

ures. His earliest masterpiece, the first of his two piano concertos, provoked at its initial performance not merely journalistic condemnations but outright hissing. Still, Brahms plodded on.

Indeed, "plodding on" sums up his whole attitude to the world. Not for him Liszt's frenetic oscillations between sanctity and devilry, nor Wagner's compulsive philosophizing. Having grown up poor and unhappy in Hamburg, Brahms moved to Vienna in his late twenties and generally stayed there. The most dramatic event of his later career was the growth, in 1878, of that majestically unkempt beard which dominated his physiognomy thereafter. This humdrum existence had no room for a wife. Scholars dispute how much truth rests in the frequent allegations (which he himself fueled) that he had spent his teens as a pianist in Hamburg's waterfront brothels; at any rate, his misogynistic and misanthropic strains increased with time. He could, and did, end alliances of years' standing with a solitary shattering taunt. Clara alone never disappointed him.

His unease with ordinary human emotion—"Passions," he sententiously assured Clara, "are not natural to mankind"—went with an intensified disquiet at overt musical emotion. In youth he signed a manifesto denouncing Liszt, Wagner, and their so-called "New German School." Subsequently, he himself treated Wagner with wary tolerance, yet the battle lines between Brahms's supporters and Wagner's proved impassable. Brahmsians considered Wagner a preposterous fraud. Wagnerians considered Brahms a timorous bore. Today we can appreciate both composers' respective greatnesses; but such disinterested insight could not be achieved then, least of all among such party-line Brahmsians as the critic Eduard Hanslick, who publicly acclaimed Brahms while privately finding his output tiresome.

In any discussion of that output, the adjective "autumnal" unavoidably figures. Even Brahms's concertos, for all the severe technical problems they pose interpreters, have hardly any animal high spirits. As a songwriter he excelled in gravitas, of which the *Alto Rhapsody* and *Four Serious Songs* are particularly intense examples. His late piano works, notably the *Rhapsodies* and *Intermezzos*, approach Liszt in their complexity (not least rhythmic complexity), while striking much deeper. The phrase used of King Lear applies just as fittingly to the much less grandiose Brahms: "Ripeness is all."

※

HOWEVER RESTRAINED BRAHMS'S latter-day conduct toward Wagner, he showed no such caution regarding Bruckner, whom he described as "deranged" and "a swindle." He dismissed Bruckner's nine mature symphonies (two student efforts stayed in manuscript) as "symphonic boa-constrictors": "One cannot make head or tail of these things, one cannot even discuss them. Nor him as a person." Party politics had blocked all hopes of musical understanding, because Bruckner idolized Wagner. Even without this circumstance, Brahms the religiously tepid city man would probably have despised Bruckner the Catholic *naïf* from rural Austria. Viennese gossip abounded concerning Bruckner's extreme simplicity: the black homespun peasant clothes he wore everywhere; his giving a coin to a conductor friend and telling him, "Take this and drink a mug of beer to my health"; his penchant for proposing marriage to women he scarcely knew; his plea to Emperor Franz Josef, "Oh Your Majesty, please stop that man Hanslick from writing horrible things about me." Yet those who looked (as Brahms seldom did) past Bruckner's bumpkin exterior found much to admire. When Bruckner undertook an organ examination, one judge commented: "This man should be examining *us*." In accordance with his unworldly detachment, he talked of his Maker with the utmost frankness: "He [God] will say: 'Why else have I given you talent, you son of a bitch, than that you should sing My praise and glory?'"

The diffidence that forever gnawed at Bruckner made him revise many of his symphonies, these revisions having become a minefield for subsequent editors, who have quarreled as to which amendments are musically justified and which were forced on him by outside opinion. In his dozens of wonderful sacred works, strangely enough, he avoided such tinkering, seeming to gain fortitude from the Palestrina heritage of choral polyphony that meant so much to him. Paradoxically, the sacred works derive recognizably from the same pen as the symphonies. All are grave, solemn, short on vivacity (Vienna's wits called Bruckner "the *Adagio* composer"), apt to halt in portentous silences, clearly influenced by Wagner, but in no respect a mere imitation. Let Bruckner have the final, laconic words: "They want me to compose in a different way: I could, but I must not."

If Bruckner aroused widespread derision, his fellow Viennese Johann Strauss Jr.—"The Waltz King"—aroused uniform affection. His one real antagonist had been his father, Johann Sr. (1804–49), who did his utmost (sometimes with a whip) to dissuade Johann Jr. from a musical livelihood. Such paternal methods had so little effect that Johann Jr. set up his own dance orchestra, in opposition to his father's, and became the toast of Vienna by the age of nineteen. One newspaper celebrated his triumph by running perhaps the most blandly murderous headline in music criticism's whole history: "Good evening, Father Strauss. Good morning, Son Strauss." Henceforth Son Strauss's career flourished. His adulthood's chronicle is little more than a list of concert tours (an 1872 visit to America brought him $100,000) and his most sensational hits: *The Blue Danube*; *The Emperor Waltz*; *Tales From The Vienna Woods*; *The Tritsch-Tratsch Polka*; *Wine, Women and Song* (a special favorite of Wagner's, perhaps in view of its title); the operettas *Die Fledermaus* and *The Gypsy Baron*; and so on and on. (The collected edition of his dances runs to fifty-one CD volumes.) Brahms is supposed to have responded to an autograph request by scribbling a few bars from a Strauss waltz and adding to it the words "Unfortunately, not by Johannes Brahms."

❧

DURING THE NINETEENTH century's first half, France had lagged behind Germany and Italy in terms of its own composers. Berlioz alone had been a front-rank native figure. This changed around 1850, when a clutch of younger Frenchmen, occasionally born outside France's borders, appeared. Among the foreigners, Jacques Offenbach (1819–80), of German-Jewish origin, became Paris's equivalent to Johann Strauss: a rare master of froth and fun who purveyed *risqué* but fundamentally good-natured satire against government and classical myth in such operettas as *Orpheus in the Underworld*, *The Grand Duchess of Gérolstein*, and *La Belle Hélène*. Unlike most clowns who long to play Hamlet, Offenbach actually succeeded, producing late in life (and dying before the première of) the unrelievedly somber *Tales of Hoffmann*.

The stage had by this time become as obsessive a taste for French musicians as it had for Italians, and many of Offenbach's French contemporaries concentrated upon it. Charles Gounod (1818–93) acquired international celebrity with his Goethe-derived opera *Faust* (1859). After a slow start, *Faust* became one of the four or five most popular operas ever written (small comfort to Gounod himself, who had ill-advisedly sold the rights to his score for a flat fee), and within thirty-six years it was performed two thousand times in Paris alone; only after the Second World War did it fade from view. Gounod also specialized in religious music of excessive glucose levels, largely unsung nowadays except for the indestructible *Ave Maria* that he confected from the first prelude of Bach's *Well-Tempered Clavier.*

Three younger men showed that Gounod had commendable successors in the next generation. Léo Delibes (1836–91) created two noteworthy ballets, *Coppélia* and *Sylvia,* as well as the opera *Lakmé,* which after early acclaim fell into neglect until British Airways employed a duet from it in a 1990s television commercial. Jules Massenet (1842–1912) shared Gounod's musical refinement—spiteful humorists called him "Gounod's daughter"—and added hints of Wagner, as well as a pathos of his own, this mixture being readily apparent in the three most performed among his two dozen operas: *Manon, Werther,* and *Thaïs.* His rival Georges Bizet (1838–75) possessed a fiercer, more voluptuous muse: early manifested in *The Pearl Fishers* (best remembered for its tenor-baritone duet *"Au fond du temple saint"*), confirmed in his incidental music to the play *L'Arlesienne,* and overwhelmingly validated in *Carmen.* With *Carmen,* Bizet achieved the remarkable feat of being censured by the French for sexual license. Well before the opera became globally treasured, Bizet had died at thirty-seven.

Meanwhile, numerous Frenchmen, instead of focusing on the theater, devoted themselves mainly to orchestral music, chamber music, keyboard music (sometimes for organ as well as for piano), and songs. Édouard Lalo (1823–92), violinist as well as composer, is known predominantly through his *Symphonie Espagnole* (a violin concerto, for all practical purposes). César

Franck (1822–90), a more vivid figure, originally came not from France but from Liège in eastern Belgium; this background helped determine his idiom's somewhat un-French earnestness. A reluctant adolescent virtuoso, Franck later fled the limelight for the much quieter role of church organist. His twelve principal organ pieces are among the most inspired since Bach. From his fifties, he bloomed anew as a creator; masterworks from his final years include his *Symphony* (which Gounod disparaged as "an affirmation of incompetence pushed to dogmatic lengths"), his *Prelude, Chorale and Fugue* for piano, his *Violin Sonata*, and his *Piano Quintet*. He also taught harmony at the Paris Conservatoire. There his great natural piety and sartorial gaucherie drew comparisons with Bruckner; there, too, his pedagogical skills earned him the keen admiration of several followers.

These followers, including Emmanuel Chabrier (1841–94), Henri Duparc (1848–1933), Vincent d'Indy (1851–1931), and Ernest Chausson (1855–99), were widely dubbed "*la Franck-maçonnerie*" (a pun on the French word for "freemasonry"). Chabrier exhibited manic gusto, evident above all in his symphonic poem *España* and his irrepressible comic opera *Le Roi Malgré Lui*. Duparc is important primarily for his fourteen delicate, rich, and superbly atmospheric songs, all the more precious in that a nervous collapse during his late thirties brought his composing to a premature end. D'Indy wrote Franck's first biography and engaged not solely in composition (where his reputation rests mainly on the *Symphony on a French Mountain Song*) but in powerful polemics. Chausson took a sensuously elegiac approach, at its best in his famous *Poème* (for violin and orchestra) and in his less known song-cycle *Poème de l'Amour et de la Mer* (two lines from this cycle encapsulate Chausson's whole spirit: "The time of lilacs and the time of roses, / Along with our love, is dead forever"). It was as if he had foretold his early demise, which occurred in a stupid cycling accident.

Opposed to *la Franck-maçonnerie,* but sharing its musical seriousness, stood Camille Saint-Saëns (1835–1921) and his loyal student Gabriel Fauré (1845–1924). Saint-Saëns, a child prodigy of Mozartian and Mendelssohnian endowments—he began playing the piano when only two years old, and composing when only three— could perform all of Beethoven's sonatas from memory at the age of ten. Perhaps so freakishly gifted a lad would inevitably experience sorrow as an adult; embittered he certainly was, with a Brahmsian sharpness of tongue, despite the official honors heaped on him (including his own statue). Though he produced over 150 superbly crafted compositions in every genre, he never succeeded in silencing accusations that he had squandered his immense natural abilities. Among his outstanding works are five piano concertos, the *Organ Symphony* (the finale from which crops up in *Babe*'s soundtrack), the *Carnival of the Animals*, the symphonic poem *Danse Macabre*, and his one commercially successful opera, *Samson and Delilah*. Such human warmth as Saint-Saëns felt for an adult revolved mostly around Fauré, who appears at his finest in his piano pieces (these, like Chopin's, mostly bear generic titles: *Nocturnes, Barcarolles, Impromptus*) and in his songs (fairly conventional early on, but afterwards plumbing exceptional depths of poetic sensitivity). Fauré's most celebrated single utterance is his *Requiem*, much more subdued than Berlioz's or Verdi's and the product of an agnostic concerned with human consolation rather than divine judgment. Another popular Fauré favorite, the *Pavane*, condenses his supple and courtly manner into five minutes' exquisite Gallic wistfulness, which is devoid of that Lisztian-Wagnerian chromaticism which *la Franck-maçonnerie* often cultivated.

۶

SAINT-SAËNS'S ITCH for travel took him to Russia, and he made new Russian music better known to the West. Musically, Russia had long been largely *terra incognita*: it had hardly any secular art music at all until the late eighteenth century, when Catherine the Great aided local musicians and imported Italian ones. Its first locally born composer of consequence, Mikhail Glinka (1804–57), made his name with two operas: *A Life for the Tsar* (1836), still occasionally revived, and *Ruslan and Ludmila* (1842), now recalled solely for its bumptious, terpsichorean overture. Today, even in his native country, he is far more read about than heard. But his Russian contemporaries and immediate successors viewed him as a second Beethoven.

Glinka's most obvious heirs constituted a group known as the *Kuchka*, which is variously translated as "Russian Five," "Mighty Five," or "Mighty Handful." This quintet consisted, strictly speaking, of amateurs: its founder, Mily Balakirev (1837–1910), earned his living as a railroad official; Alexander Borodin (1833–87) became a respected chemist; Modest Musorgsky (1839–81) occupied various government clerkships; Nikolai Rimsky-Korsakov (1844–1908) joined the navy; and César Cui (1835–1918), by far the least important member, worked as a military engineer. In place of conventional tuition came edicts from Balakirev, who, between bouts of characteristically Slavic religious mania, nagged his friends into writing the types of music he wanted. His own output, small and haphazard, remains almost wholly obscure except for his awesomely difficult piano barnstormer *Islamey.*

At least Borodin's chemistry professorship gave him an excuse for his musical underproduction. He seldom had time to compose unless illness postponed his chemistry lectures, or unless he had temporarily vanquished his wife's mania for allowing her cats—not to mention bohemian relatives and friends—to inflict domestic havoc. Not surprisingly, Borodin took five years to finish his first symphony and seven to finish his rightly famous second (probably the best thing he ever wrote). He never did finish his opera *Prince Igor*, which had to be completed after his death.

Borodin derived contentment from hard science; Musorgsky, deficient in Borodin's intellectual acuity, dreamed of salvation from vodka bottles. His early song, "Ah, You Drunken Sot," proved an impressively accurate memoir. We know most of Musorgsky's pieces because others, notably Rimsky-Korsakov, thought enough of them to edit them for publication and performing. No other composer has shared Musorgsky's reliance on later musicians' willingness to save him from himself. His suite *Pictures at an Exhibition*, a contender for history's least idiomatic piano work, required subsequent orchestral alchemy to reveal its potential. A man who regularly leaves his largest compositions unperformably incomplete or, in the case of his main opera *Boris Godunov*, finishes them twice over (neither version being, in practice, stageable without alterations taken from the other, or without other hands' interventions), is a man fairly determined upon artistic self-destruction. His booze-sodden dementia startled even the most indulgent elements of that officialdom which protractedly employed him and eventually dismissed him. *Boris* excepted, Musorgsky's ambition accorded with his actual accomplishment in domestic vocal works alone. His three song-cycles, *The Nursery*, *Songs and Dances of Death*, and *Sunless,* reveal mastery of the grotesque at the expense of almost all other features.

Rimsky-Korsakov had too neat and industrious a mind to imitate Musorgsky's noble-savage primitivism or Borodin's irresolution. After leaving the navy he astonished himself by obtaining a chair in composition at Saint Petersburg's Conservatoire, although none knew better than he his own shortcomings. By concentrated hard work, he learned enough about music theory's rules—of which Balakirev's hectoring encyclicals had left him largely unaware—to ensure that he could teach his pupils something. His newfound erudition chagrined Balakirev, who increasingly considered him a decadent pro-Western renegade. Actually Rimsky-Korsakov harbored an ardent love for Russian folklore, musical and otherwise; he simply appreciated the pitfalls of untrained dilettantish enthusiasm. Best remembered today for his orchestral classics, scored with the most beguiling coloristic sense (especially *Capriccio Espagnol* and *Scheherazade*), he himself took most pride in his fifteen operas, which show his preoccupation with the supernatural. One such opera, *The Golden Cockerel,* supplemented this preoccupation with lampoons of Tsarism's martial bungling lampoons couched in fey language, but sufficiently sharp to preclude any performance of the work in Rimsky-Korsakov's lifetime.

❧

SHARING IN CONCENTRATED form Rimsky-Korsakov's musical fastidiousness, Peter Ilyich Tchaikovsky (1840–93) combined it with a temperament highly strung and despondent from childhood ("if it had not been for music, I should have gone mad"). Tchaikovsky's greatest inspirations—marked by an extreme melodic fertility, a knack for apposite orchestration, and a much-underrated architectural sense—include the six symphonies; the ballets *Swan Lake, Sleeping Beauty,* and *The Nutcracker*; the fantasy overture *Romeo and Juliet*; and the opera *Eugene*

Onegin. It is surprising how many of these compositions originally met cold or downright hostile responses. Only in later years did he obtain some artistic satisfaction, when an eccentric millionairess named Nadezha von Meck gave him six thousand rubles annually, on condition that donor and recipient never met. After thirteen years, Madame von Meck suddenly ended the pension, thus confirming Tchaikovsky in his despairing view of humankind. This view had already been strengthened by his catastrophic marriage, which lasted but nine weeks (an object lesson in the perils of appeasing an erotomaniacal stalker), and by his impatience with most contemporaries: he called Musorgsky's oeuvre "the lowest, commonest parody of music," said of Borodin that "he cannot write a line without outside help," and referred to Brahms as "a talentless bastard." Of Mozart's genius, by contrast, Tchaikovsky never wearied. His death remains controversial. Maybe he killed himself—he had probably attempted to kill himself after fleeing his wife—but it is much likelier that he perished from mere imprudence in drinking unboiled water amid a cholera epidemic. What is certain is that the now-fashionable interpretation of Tchaikovsky as a "gay martyr" destroyed by "homophobic" society springs from Anglo-American parochialism. Homosexual males had a much easier time in Tsarist Russia than in Oscar Wilde's Britain (let alone under the Soviets); Tchaikovsky's own homosexual tastes, far from being thought unspeakably scandalous, were tolerated and often shared at the highest reaches of government.

常

RUSSIA'S EMERGENCE AS a leading musical power coincided with the similar emergence of several other countries, mostly outside the main musical currents of preceding centuries: Bohemia (now in the Czech Republic), Norway, Denmark, Finland, Spain, and England. Textbooks always refer to these countries' leading nineteenth- and early twentieth-century composers as "nationalists." This is misleading: such composers are better described as patriots. They were motivated, after all, by love of their homelands, not—as is the nationalist—by contempt toward others' homelands.

As Glinka became the father of Russian music, so Bedřich Smetana (1824–84) became the father of Czech music. An excellent pianist, he received encouragement from Liszt but achieved more success in his directorship of Prague's Czech National Theater, for which he wrote ten operas. Of these, *The Bartered Bride,* a delectable, one-off comedy of manners and a prize instance of art concealing art, remains in the repertoire. (Every last one of *The Bartered Bride*'s spontaneous-sounding, folk-like melodies is actually an original Smetana creation.) All his other stage works are now totally overlooked, save among his countrymen. The same fate has engulfed most of his other music, though his affecting series of six symphonic poems *Má Vlast* often turns up in the world's concert halls, and his *First String Quartet* (of two) is still fairly frequently heard. Never heard by the composer, though. Aged fifty, he lost his hearing. The tinnitus that preceded this disaster is depicted with painful vividness in the quartet's finale. Eventually syphilis made him not merely deaf but also insane, and, like Schumann, he died in a madhouse.

If Smetana was Czech music's weeping philosopher, Antonín Dvořák (1841–1904) was its laughing philosopher, whose rhythmic ebullience and Tchaikovskian thematic fecundity endowed much of his output with abiding freshness. Brahms actively supported him, successfully recommending his music to the Simrock publishing house. "I shall be indebted to you all my life," Dvořák humbly assured his benefactor. More versatile than Smetana, he shone in almost every genre he undertook: nine symphonies (he misguidedly suppressed the first four), including his immortal tribute to the United States, *From The New World*; the vernally bright *Slavonic Dances*; fifteen string quartets, notably the *American Quartet* (until the 1950s British reference books unblushingly called this *The Nigger Quartet*); and the *Cello Concerto,* representing him at his most passionate ("Why," Brahms marveled, "didn't I know that one could write a cello concerto like this?"). Averse to theorizing, Dvořák—who for years played violin in the orchestra that Smetana directed—believed with simple faith in God and the Czech people. His capacity for mysticism began and ended with his addiction to watching trains go by.

Dvořák's friends included Leoš Janáček (1854–1928), who veered off to pursue very different paths. Opera, for Dvořák rather a side-issue, dominated Janáček's existence. Influenced by Musorgsky's love of the demotic, Janáček sought to give his own operas the character of spoken plays, and he noted down little quasi-melodic traits of ordinary conversation. This quest for "speech melody" became obsessive and had the effect of rendering his operas even more completely meaningless in translation than are most others. These operas, devoted to Slavic subjects, include *Jenůfa* (his first big success), *Kátya Kabanová*, *The Makropoulos Case*, and *From The House of the Dead*. Peculiarly enough, he had reached his fifties before he acquired any European fame, and his sixties before most of his main pieces were written.

᠉᠉

SWEDEN EXPERIENCED NO great musical upsurge. Its one significant nineteenth-century composer, Franz Berwald (1796–1868), cultivated an approach both too unconventional and insufficiently folkloric to inflame national pride, though his four symphonies indicate his harmonic initiative and metric ingenuity. Matters were very different elsewhere in Scandinavia.

Norway, for instance (which did not shake off Swedish control till 1905), produced Edvard Grieg (1843–1907). Modest, unaffected, and companionable in art and life alike, Grieg stuck mostly to miniatures. There his distinct, succulent harmonic style—so distinct that he sometimes seemed its slave rather than its master—could shine. Of his best-known pieces only the *Piano*

Concerto, which Liszt played superbly at sight ("An old hand like me ought to manage a bit of sight-reading, don't you think?"), essays a large-scale form. Otherwise, Grieg's bigger works—*Peer Gynt*; the *Holberg Suite* for strings; the song-cycle *Haugtussa*—usually consisted of small works strung together, very elegantly at that. His knowledge of Norwegian folk music grew exhaustive, his imaginative sympathy with it acute. Like most essentially epigrammatic artists, he is all too easy to take for granted. He deplored his own commercial acclaim: "It is surely no fault of mine that my music is heard in third-rate hotels and from schoolgirls." There are worse destinies.

Denmark's Carl Nielsen (1865–1931) lacked Grieg's popular touch, although the same Nordic breezes that wafted through Grieg's harmonies can occasionally be detected in Nielsen's. Moreover, Nielsen, for all his devotion to Danish culture, concerned himself with epic gestures such as Grieg largely eschewed. Six symphonies dominate Nielsen's achievement. He made a habit of "progressive tonality"—in other words, starting a piece in one key and finishing it in another—not through any vagueness but, on the contrary, for heightened dramatic impact. Indeed, though both his own operas are seldom heard, he recurrently seems to be a dramatist despite himself. The violent *coups de théâtre* in his symphonies include the finale of the Fourth (where two timpanists antiphonally brawl at the movement's climax) and that of the Fifth (where a side-drum repeatedly interrupts the prevailing shouts of orchestral exultation). His chamber-music, including the *Wind Quintet*, is less distinctive.

Nielsen shared his year of birth, and his aptitude for heroic orchestral thinking, with Finland's greatest musician: Sibelius. Yet the two composers had little else in

---

SIBELIUS, JEAN (JULIUS CHRISTIAN) (Finnish, 1865–1957). The time is long past, we hope, when strenuously modish critics—like the logorrheic Marxist T. W. Adorno—could dismiss Sibelius as a provincial bungler, a kind of musical Grandma Moses hopelessly outclassed by *real* progressives. For an alleged provincial bungler, he has taken a long time to fade away. During his late twenties he found his compositional voice, personal and obstinately memorable. Possessing in his best music the rare gift of inspiring awe without needing to shout, he was at his most consistently impressive in his seven symphonies and in his tone poems, not that the two genres were always readily distinguishable in his hands. Whereas numerous contemporaries piled detail on detail, Sibelius pared detail after detail away till the results were as stark, rough-hewn, and heroic as Stonehenge. And like Stonehenge, his output supplies (as his British biographer Robert Layton observed) "the illusion that it has always been in existence." Exceedingly famous is his early tone poem *Finlandia*, a protest against Russian occupation, and one accordingly banned by both the Tsarist and Soviet regimes. Better introductions to Sibelius, however, are *The Swan of Tuonela*, a mostly string-accompanied English horn solo of piercing beauty; the *Fourth Symphony*, with its ending of unsurpassed desolation; the *Fifth Symphony*, as jubilant as its predecessor is bleak; and the Swedish-language threnody *S'en har jag ej frågat mera* (*Since Then I Have Questioned No Further*), which shows that Sibelius the songwriter ranks with several figures much more famous than he in vocal music. Even during his lifetime his portrait adorned Finnish postage stamps; and on the day he turned ninety, he received twelve thousand telegrams as

common. Nielsen (like Grieg) possessed a primarily humanistic worldview. Sibelius's worldview seldom appears concerned by humanity at all, so wholly is it suffused with a spirit of pantheism, of "old unhappy far-off things," of vast obdurate landscapes. Much more significant in his outlook than the conventional musical training he had in Germany was the *Kalevala*, a storehouse of Finnish legend to which he repeatedly turned for inspiration. Even when his music did not specifically cite *Kalevala* tales (which it did in such pieces as *Kullervo, Four Legends,* and *Pohjola's Daughter*), the mood of ancient sagas predominated, explaining his tendency to titles like *En Saga, Night-Ride and Sunrise,* and *The Bard*. In his last (1926) **tone poem**, *Tapiola*—Tapio being, in the *Kalevala*, the forest-god—Sibelius managed a devastating, elemental fury of utterance that scares even legend away. Following *Tapiola*, his natural inclination to self-doubt (possibly unavoidable with so wintry and taciturn an artist, who correctly likened his *Sixth Symphony* to "pure cold water") overwhelmed him. Though he came close to reaching his ninety-second birthday, after his mid-sixties he wrote precious little; he burned a long-promised eighth symphony before anyone could see it. The last pre-*Tapiola* major work he published had been, appropriately, music for a production of *The Tempest*, where, like Prospero, he

---

well as a box of cigars from Churchill. His brooding visage, cast in stainless steel, overlooks a Helsinki park: an appropriate tribute to one who commented, "Nobody ever put up a statue to a critic."

seems to bid a resigned farewell to his enchantments. During the very period when Sibelius began explaining Finland to foreigners, new musical life burgeoned at the continent's opposite end. Spain, devoid for centuries of native musicians known abroad, suddenly produced three of them: Isaac Albéniz (1860–1909), Enrique Granados (1867–1916), and Manuel de Falla (1876–1946).

Albéniz, who studied piano with Liszt (no less) after a picaresque boyhood worthy of any Spanish novelist, warrants notice mainly for his exhibitionistic suite *Iberia*: a prize example of the no-holds-barred, twenty-fingers-on-each-hand pianistic tradition. Granados provided his own answer to *Iberia* in *Goyescas*, a slightly more restrained work—written to pay Goya homage—which its composer afterwards turned into an opera. Returning from the operatic *Goyescas*'s New York première, Granados drowned when submarine action sank his ship. One British critic memorably called Granados "a refined and gentle soul who might have been . . . slowly destroyed by events had a torpedo not achieved the result more summarily." Falla owed something to Albéniz in the riotous hues of his earlier successes (*Nights in the Gardens of Spain, The Three-Cornered Hat*), then switched to a far more ascetic manner (best exemplified by his *Harpsichord Concerto*) that evoked sixteenth-century Spanish mysticism.

※

ENGLISHMEN HAVE RARELY felt flattered by comparisons with Spaniards, but England as well as Spain somehow

lost the art of producing widely renowned native composers during the eighteenth and early nineteenth centuries.
So when Sir Arthur Sullivan (1842–1900) earned himself
immortality through the "Savoy Operas" on which he
collaborated with playwright W. S. Gilbert, he became
the most eminent English-born musician since Purcell.
Even the shortest list of Gilbert and Sullivan triumphs
must include *The Mikado, The Pirates of Penzance, H.M.S.
Pinafore, Iolanthe, Trial by Jury,* and *The Gondoliers.* How
curious, therefore, that Sullivan (along with numerous
sober-sided contemporaries) considered his comic mastery somewhat disgraceful and longed—particularly after
his knighthood—for recognition as a "serious" composer.
It was as if Johann Strauss had craved all his life to be
Wagner, or as if Rossini had yearned to be Beethoven.

A younger English composer eventually had greater
success than Sullivan at getting his own serious aims
acknowledged: the largely self-taught Sir Edward Elgar (1857–1934), whose birth's 2007 sesquicentenary
unleashed in England a veritable avalanche of remembrance. For every music-lover who knows Elgar's biggest
and subtlest works (the two symphonies, the symphonic
poem *Falstaff,* the violin and cello concertos, the *Enigma
Variations,* the oratorio *The Dream of Gerontius*), a thousand know his *Pomp and Circumstance Marches:* the first
of which, originally wordless, was fitted to the text of
Land of Hope and Glory at the instigation of Elgar's royal
friend Edward VII. Far from being ashamed of it, Elgar
called it "a damned fine popular tune," which it is.

While Elgar had deflected querying about folk music by his defiant self-description "I am folk music," other musicians took more seriously than he that treasury of English folksong which, in the early twentieth century, seemed likely to disappear. Frederick Delius (1862–1934) keenly felt the attractions of (and periodically alluded to) such song in a peripatetic career that took him to both Florida and France; he spent his later years—thanks to venereal disease—blind and paralyzed, compelled to dictate his final music to his faithful amanuensis and fellow Yorkshireman Eric Fenby. Folk song meant, if anything, still more to Gustav Holst (1874–1934); yet he suffered the sad fate of being famous for only one work, the kaleidoscopic orchestral suite *The Planets*. Holst's friend Ralph Vaughan Williams (1872–1958) bathed in such folk song, allowing its melodic features to penetrate his innermost creative processes, though he seldom quoted it outright. With this great musical love he combined an equal love for sixteenth-century music, and one of his most enduringly popular pieces is his early *Fantasia on a Theme of Thomas Tallis*. His compositional life stretched until the 1950s and included nine symphonies as well as much choral music and half a dozen stage works, but his individual tone had already become observable well before World War I.

※

HOLST SHARED HIS one-hit-wonder status with several turn-of-the-century Italian composers, above all Pietro Mascagni (1863–1945) and Ruggiero Leoncavallo (1857–1919). Mascagni burst into the headlines with his 1890 opera *Cavalleria Rusticana*, Leoncavallo with his opera *Pagliacci* two years afterwards. Not only did each composer fail to gain equal success with anything else he wrote, but each hit is usually performed as part of a double-bill with the other, this conjunction later inspiring Ogden Nash's cleverest rhyme: "His chin was scratchy / He felt as lonely as *Cavalleria* without *Pagliacci*." Giacomo Puccini (1858–1924), determined to avoid the mistake of shooting his own bolt when young, won a far more enduring esteem; four of his operas—*La Bohème, Tosca, Madama Butterfly,* and the posthumously finished *Turandot*—are among the most widely staged of all time. Laboring with agonized slowness, he aimed at perfection and frequently reached it, helped thither by melodic genius, splendid workmanship, and a flair (which Verdi seldom had till late in life) for nagging his librettists into excelling themselves. In recent years Puccini's lesser known operas, such as *Manon Lescaut, La Fanciulla del West*, and *Il Trittico*, have approached the Big Four in popularity.

Turandot's Chinese subject matter had already attracted others, especially the Italian-born but Germanicized scholar-pianist-composer Ferruccio Busoni (1866–1924), who lacked Puccini's theatrical finesse. Busoni showed himself to better advantage in his abundant piano music, which often consciously refers to Bach and Liszt, aiming at the former's polyphonic elaboration and the latter's virtuoso skills. Some of it consists simply of Bach arrangements. Probably his two most important productions were his *Fantasia Contrappuntistica*—usually played, when played at all, in its solo piano rather than its subsequent two-piano version—and his incomplete opera *Doktor Faust.* Both works (though Busoni considered himself a "young classicist") flaunt an ultra-Romantic diablerie; but it is a strangely *cold* diablerie, the opposite of Liszt's surging self-confidence.

❧

AMONG BUSONI'S NUMEROUS German and Austrian contemporaries must be named Engelbert Humperdinck (1854–1921), whose opera *Hansel and Gretel* endures unscathed by time; Hugo Wolf (1860–1903), the tortured, ferociously Wagnerian composer of almost 250 songs, frequently superb, who ended his erratic life in a mental home; Max Reger (1873–1916), best known for his organ music; Hans Pfitzner (1869–1949), noted principally for his opera *Palestrina*, an imaginative treatment of that composer's career; and Gustav Mahler (1860–1911), the most cosmically ambitious of the four. The nine symphonies Mahler finished were all written according to the formula that he announced in a 1907 conversation with Sibelius: "A symphony should be like the world, it must contain everything." Most of Mahler's run to great length—the first movement of his Third takes more than half an hour to perform—but are episodic rather than coherent, particularly where (following the precedent of Beethoven's Ninth) he uses voices, as in the Second, Third, Fourth and Eighth. Nor does his fondness for banal melodic invention—to which he generally imparts a knowing, self-conscious quality, quite different from, say, Liszt's lapses into cheerful triteness—often disappear. His best things reside in his song-cycles with orchestra: *Lieder eines Fahrenden Gesellen*, *Kindertotenlieder*, and above all *Das Lied von der Erde*, where he achieves a delicacy of touch for which the symphonies do little to prepare anyone.

In his own day Mahler's conducting brought him much greater recognition than his composing; and as a creator he remained in the shadow of his slightly younger colleague Richard Strauss. Before his thirtieth birthday

---

STRAUSS, RICHARD (GEORG) (German, 1864–1949). Unrelated to Johann Strauss, although he much admired the latter and alluded to him in his great 1911 comedy *Der Rosenkavalier*. (An anonymous clerihew has it: "Johann Strauss / Composed *Die Fledermaus* / But Richard Strauss wrote properer / Opera.") Richard had one of the longest creative spans of any composer who ever lived: his earliest works (bland but unfailingly professional) date from his childhood, his last from more than seventy years later. Endowed with a phenomenal technique that often expressed itself in dizzyingly intricate orchestral textures, he was repeatedly charged in his own day with "decadence"—as meaningless a term as "formalism" would be under Soviet Communists—and never ceased to rile the puritan tendency apt to lurk in numerous ostentatiously progressive souls. His taste for musical autobiography, generally tongue-in-cheek (a taste most apparent in two orchestral epics, *Ein Heldenleben* and *Sinfonia Domestica*), created particular scandal. Unlike most of his musical contemporaries, Strauss became a millionaire, investing

Strauss had become a world-renowned *enfant terrible,* his gorgeously orchestrated symphonic poems *Till Eulenspiegel, Don Juan, Thus Spake Zarathustra,* and *Don Quixote* (to name but four) outraging and delighting audiences in about equal measure. Today Strauss's stylistic debts to his forebears, especially Liszt and Wagner, are conspicuous; but in his youth he seemed the wildest of iconoclasts. If his earlier orchestral works inspired alarm, the one-act operas *Salome* and *Elektra* gave him the widespread reputation of an outright pornographer, goading Kaiser Wilhelm II into a typically inaccurate prediction: "I really like this fellow Strauss, but *Salome* will do him terrible damage." This "damage" consisted, in practice, of royalties that flowed like wine, particularly when *Der Rosenkavalier* showed his urbane geniality. After World

---

cannily, living frugally, and even *looking* like the quiet, unobtrusive businessman that he was. His post-*Rosenkavalier* stage works, including *Ariadne auf Naxos, Arabella,* and *Capriccio,* tend to be connoisseurs' pieces; but if musical beauty were the sole criterion for operatic success, they would be standard fare. Despite his lack of formal education, he had a keen instinct for literary worth in the libretti he used, and two of his operatic collaborators were important authors in their own right: Hugo von Hofmannsthal and Stefan Zweig. The fallacy that Strauss's post-1918 powers declined has now been deservedly scotched; it never had much more basis than critical vexation at his reluctance to follow certain juniors on the road to thoroughgoing dissonance. His old age is an inspiration to us all, producing as it did the rapturous *Four Last Songs* (among the greatest song-cycles since Schubert's), and a witticism deserving commemoration: "I'm not a first-rate composer, but I'm a first-rate second-rate composer."

War I, Germany's artistic environment underwent such seismic changes as to rob Strauss of his firebrand status; and while much of his greatest music lay ahead, he forfeited his earlier shock value.

That shock value Arnold Schoenberg (1874–1951) abundantly retained. Schoenberg had taken music lessons from his brother-in-law Alexander Zemlinsky (1871–1942), a figure of at least comparable gifts—Zemlinsky's *Lyric Symphony* is an authentic debauch of melancholy *Art Nouveau* arabesque—but he was otherwise still more completely autodidactic than Strauss. His early pieces, which in all honesty give greater satisfaction than most of his subsequent ones, exhibit Strauss's impact: *Verklärte Nacht* (for strings), and *Gurrelieder* (a cantata scored for huge forces and making almost unheard-of demands on singers and players). Afterwards he cultivated tonal freedom increasingly for its own sake, the best-known result being his song-cycle *Pierrot Lunaire*, a protracted exploration of atonality: that is, music deficient in any sense of key. (Schoenberg himself preferred speaking of "pantonality," but this term never caught on.) *Pierrot Lunaire*'s other most prevalent trait—also briefly employed in *Gurrelieder*—is its use of *Sprechstimme* (speech-song), where the vocal pitches are to be merely touched on rather than sung. As a study in expressionist single-mindedness *Pierrot Lunaire* has its importance; but few have ever wished it longer. Messianic in temperament, Schoenberg resembled his fellow modernist obsessive Ezra Pound rather than a corrosive modernist cynic like Picasso. He nevertheless had some humor, whether self-serving ("My music isn't 'modern,' it's just badly played") or self-deprecating. In the Austrian army a superior asked him "Are you the *composer* Schoenberg?" "Somebody had to be," he replied, "and no one else wanted the job."

❧

"Music without *Sauerkraut*." Such was the wish of France's Erik Satie (1866–1925), as expressed to his friend Debussy. Both men chafed under the German compositional heritage, which to Strauss and Schoenberg meant so much. But each man dealt with this heritage in a different way. Satie created his own parallel universe of facetiousness (many of his works bore such names as *Desiccated Embryos*), Rosicrucianism, bohemianism, and—inscrutably—the fanatical acquisition of umbrellas. His best-known pieces are the early *Gymnopédies* (No. 1 of which has been exploited almost to death by now) and *Gnossiennes*; in these he brought something new to music, mainly because of his extreme fondness for the old melodic modes that the late seventeenth century's establishment of the major-minor key system had pretty much banished. Debussy always looked on him with fondness.

Debussy, Claude (-Achille) (French, 1862–1918). He shall be associated forever by the public with the term "impressionism," which he disdained when applied to himself. Defiantly chauvinistic ("were there fifty million Boches, French thought is indestructible," he once snarled), he proclaimed his opposition to Wagner and had

Few other musicians enjoyed Debussy's goodwill. A voluptuary who never lost his champagne tastes, although he mostly lived on a beer income, Debussy had a formidable power for ridicule and little compunction about revealing it. In cadging money from friends, he followed Wagner's example. Scornful of the conventional pedagogy he received at the Paris Conservatoire, he was once asked by an exasperated teacher what harmonic rules he supposed himself to be following: to which query he responded, *"Mon plaisir."* Always standoffish, he once wrote: "The masses can no more be ordered to love beauty than they can be persuaded to walk around on their hands." He might have been like many another

———————————————

little time for even Beethoven, preferring Couperin and Rameau to either. He adored the piano, whose literature he enriched with such collections as *Pour Le Piano,* two books of *Preludes,* and one book of *Etudes.* There he lavishly explored the veiled, half-lit sonorities that the instrument's sustaining pedal offered (his pianistic ideal, he said, would be "an instrument without hammers"). When writing for the orchestra he avoided conventional symphonic and concerto genres, concentrating, instead, on tone poems: notably *Prélude pour l'Après-midi d'un Faune, Images, Nocturnes* (these last based on the paintings of Whistler), and *La Mer.* For years he worked as a newspaper music critic—impatient and often abusive—under the pen name "Monsieur Croche." His opera *Pelléas et Mélisande* echoes (paradoxically in view of its composer's own tastes) Wagner's cultivation of legend but is as reserved and understated as Wagner's own operas are epic and vehement. Congenitally hedonistic, an incorrigible womanizer, Debussy achieved the remarkable feat of driving both his first wife *and* a mistress to shoot themselves, in separate incidents, when he dumped them; both survived their injuries.

indolent purveyor of Nietzschean clichés but for his extraordinarily acute inner ear. From early in life he knew the sort of music he wished to write, and in his dogged, surly fashion he proved a revolutionist. One of his stylistic trademarks is the whole-tone scale, which he did not invent (Glinka had occasionally used it), but which he found indispensable. The whole-tone scale, as its name indicates, dispenses with major and minor scales' mixture of tones and semitones; it consists of the notes C-D-E-F sharp-G sharp (A flat)-A-sharp (B flat)-C or else B-C sharp-D sharp (E flat)-F-G-A-B, the result instilling a sense of harmonic indecision integral to Debussy's art. Whether writing for the piano, the string quartet, the orchestra, the ballet, or (in *Pélleas et Mélisande*) the opera house, Debussy staked his claims to posterity upon his artistic sensuousness, his un-Teutonic sense of development, and his ability to conjure up an atmosphere in a few notes.

A good and easy way of annoying Debussy consisted of lumping him with his younger contemporary Maurice Ravel (1875–1937), who, indeed, has unduly often been coupled with Debussy, rather as if the two men were like Gilbert and Sullivan or Rolls and Royce. Ravel showed Debussy great respect: "It was hearing this work [*L'Après-Midi d'un Faune*], so many years ago, that I first understood what real music was." Yet almost everything Ravel produced—including the ballets *Daphnis and Chloé* and *Mother Goose*, the early but sublime *Pavane for a Dead Infanta*, and the definitive orchestral arrangement of Musorgsky's *Pictures at an Exhibition*—has a harder-edged character than Debussy's output, is less diaphanous, more acidulous, sometimes more nightmarish, occasionally suggesting the acerbic dryness of his fellow French composer Albert Roussel (1869–1937). Such Ravel piano masterpieces as *Gaspard de la Nuit* plumb abysses of terror, as, in its much less subtle orchestral way, does the hackneyed but indispensable *Boléro*. (However many times one hears it, *Boléro*'s concluding swerve to an unrelated key retains its power to frighten. One woman at its first performance insisted "The man is mad!"; Ravel observed, "Only she realized the truth.") Withdrawn and persnickety by nature, only five feet tall, and addicted to mechanical toys, Ravel twice refused membership of France's Legion of Honor, thus prompting Satie to complain, "It is not enough to refuse the Legion of Honor. One should never have deserved it."

❧

By 1900 the idea of a Russian musician no longer seemed as odd as it did in 1850. Accordingly, younger Russians tended to be more cosmopolitan, less obsessed with folkishness at all costs, than Musorgsky and Balakirev had been. Russia had particularly close links with France, culturally as well as politically; the Russian educated classes, composers included, spoke and wrote in French.

Of all such composers, none could match the outright weirdness of Alexander Scriabin (1872–1915), a child prodigy (both pianistic and creative) who fell in love with theosophy and Chopin's music to approximately equal extents. He would even, it is said, keep Chopin works under his pillow, hoping to absorb the older man's style by nocturnal osmosis. Preoccupied with the notion of color and music (each musical key, for him, represented a different shade), Scriabin also became preoccupied with his redemptive role in the cosmos, according to which he would first show himself as World Messiah in an Indian temple. His religious writings may charitably be called insane, although the occasional extract—particularly "You are not you. I am God!"—has the virtue of concision. Alas, he died of an infected pimple on his upper lip before he could undergo Indian rebirthing. What saves him from mere fruitcake marginality is the enterprise of his best music, which ranges from youthful piano works, which indeed resemble a kind of updated Chopin, to such mature productions as the orchestral *Poem of Ecstasy* and the *White Mass* piano sonata. These use a so-called "mystic chord," but conjure up a surprising variety from such limited harmonic means.

In many respects Sergei Rachmaninoff (1873–1943) constituted Scriabin's diametrical opposite (both men studied piano with the same teacher). Rachmaninoff was as self-doubting as Scriabin was egomaniacal, as conventionally Christian as Scriabin was idiosyncratically pagan. When Rachmaninoff's *First Symphony* appeared—not helped in its path to popularity by a drunken conductor—César Cui likened it to the Seven Plagues of Egypt. Following this and other emotional torments, Rachmaninoff sank into a depression that lasted three years until a hypnotist, Nikolai Dahl, persuaded him to compose again. The immediate result, the rather neo-Tchaikovskian *Second Piano Concerto* (he wrote four altogether), became one of his most beloved works; it is approached in popularity by the *Third Piano Concerto*, the symphonic poem *The Isle of the Dead*, and a cantata called *The Bells*. Forced into European and American exile by the Bolshevik Revolution, Rachmaninoff devoted all too little subsequent time to composing, being obliged to support himself as pianist and, to a lesser extent, as conductor.

Rachmaninoff never particularly aimed to startle; Igor Stravinsky (1882–1971) never particularly aimed at anything *except* startling. A student of Rimsky-Korsakov, Stravinsky acquired international fame while still in his late twenties, when the impresario Sergei Diaghilev—in charge of the *Ballets Russes*, then electrifying audiences in Paris and, to a lesser extent, elsewhere—championed his captivating score *The Firebird*. Diaghilev understandably sought a follow-up and obtained it from Stravinsky in the shape of a much more prickly, grotesque, and consciously modernistic score, *Petrushka*. But even this caused much less consternation than the Parisian riot that occurred two years later, in 1913, at the première of Stravinsky's *The Rite of Spring*. An unrelenting exploration of polyrhythm, *The Rite* (in the words of dramatist Paul Claudel) "attacked the soul as an icy north wind or a merciless sun the body." Even now that it has become a repertory standard, it represents a punitive challenge for both conductors and orchestras. Its relentlessness, though not its garish colors, reappeared in a subsequent (1917) ballet, *Les Noces* (The Wedding), more overtly Russian than anything else in Stravinsky's entire list of pieces. No one suspected as much at the time, but Stravinsky's creative gifts had already peaked.

❧❧❧

BETWEEN THE WARS

※

W HEN NOVEMBER 1918's armistice came to a war-weary and blood-drenched Europe, there occurred a widespread sense not merely of disillusionment—that was to be expected—but of active loathing towards cultural traditions. Never has a younger generation tried harder to shock its elders than did the generation that emerged after the First World War, in music as elsewhere. Elgar, Richard Strauss, and to a lesser extent Sibelius found themselves commonly mocked as dinosaurs. The few composers from before 1914 who continued to lead fashion tended to be those (Schoenberg and Stravinsky in particular) who prided themselves on their cutting-edge modernism.

Schoenberg, intransigent still, had attracted numerous pupils even before the Great War, such as Alban Berg (1885–1935) and Anton von Webern (1883–1945). In 1923 Schoenberg announced his invention of the twelve-tone—alias dodecaphonic—method, by which (to give a grossly oversimplified but accurate summation) each of the twelve notes in the octave is accorded an equal value. This technique, he imagined with characteristic missionary optimism, "will guarantee the supremacy of German music for the next hundred years." Berg—whom Sibelius, only half in jest, called "Schoenberg's best work"—turned out to be dodecaphony's heretic, in that while using the technique he freely allowed pre-Schoenbergian tonal implications into his writing, especially his powerful *Violin Concerto*, with its Bach allusions. His opera *Wozzeck* avoids dodecaphony altogether (unsurprisingly, since he finished it a year before his teacher had proclaimed the method) and, while predominantly atonal, conveys strong tonal implications at certain points. *Lulu*, Berg's other opera, does use dodecaphony; it had to wait till 1979 for a complete performance. Webern, justifiably uncertain both of the twelve-tone method's suitability for long-term structures and of his own capacity to maintain such structures, concentrated on producing miniatures. In France, or rather in Paris (where Stravinsky spent most of the 1920s and 1930s), a more impish sort of modernism prevailed. Very little of Stravinsky's interwar music—*Pulcinella* (based closely on Pergolesi), the *Symphony of Psalms*, the *Symphonies of Wind Instruments,* and much else—shared the quality of, or even appeared to come from the same hand as, his pre-1918 achievements. He flitted from one idiom to another like (to quote one 1936 commentator) "the Flying Dutchman of Music" but unencumbered by even the slightest discernible self-doubt. "I am on a perfectly sure road. There is nothing to discuss nor to criticize. One does not criticize anybody or anything that is functioning. A nose is not manufactured: a nose just *is*. Thus, too, my art." He essayed twelve-tone procedures himself once Schoenberg died, but without thereby demonstrating a particle of Berg's flexibility with them.

The long Parisian custom of hospitality towards musical foreigners (a custom that explained Stravinsky's presence in the city) continued and had a particular impact on two composers originally from Eastern Europe: George Enescu (1881–1955), from Romania, and the Czech Bohuslav Martinů (1890–1959), the latter being the more stylistically consistent, with a special taste for motoric rhythms and bright woodwind tints. Meanwhile (also in Paris) Satie presided over, and the playwright-novelist-filmmaker Jean Cocteau acted as public relations officer for, a group of young musicians known as *Les Six*. Three of *Les Six* went on to major careers: Arthur Honegger (1892–1955), Darius Milhaud (1892–1974), and Francis Poulenc (1899–1963). Honegger, the most serious of them, showed a certain Swiss sobriety (true to his family heritage) in his five symphonies, and a certain Wagnerian amplitude in oratorios like *Joan of Arc at the Stake*. Milhaud and Poulenc went in, on the other hand, for Satie-like mischief, especially evident in Poulenc's songs, where his naturally short-breathed style worked to his advantage. All these composers, nevertheless, were thrust into the shade by the exuberant genius of a slightly younger figure: Messiaen. The greatest composer (in France and possibly anywhere else) to have emerged since Ravel's last years, Messiaen could take any technical procedures—however seemingly incompatible—and make them unquestionably his own.

※

FOREIGN COMPOSERS IN Paris between the wars included a notable contingent from the Western Hemisphere. Bra-

---

MESSIAEN, OLIVIER (French, 1908–92). Glorious, full-blooded mysticism. Saint Francis of Assisi preached to the birds, but Messiaen let the birds preach to *him*, meanwhile notating their calls with an exactitude greater than any previous composer's. Still, birdsong (one piece of his is actually called *Catalogue des Oiseaux*) formed only a part—albeit a vital part—of his style, so unremittingly colorful as to make even Scriabin and suchlike hippy-trippy precursors sound almost pallid. A lifelong Catholic who lauded sweaty desire, Messiaen cultivated from his twenties an immediately recognizable instrumental idiom: slow, hieratic brass chords, often against skittering, hyperactive xylophone and glockenspiel cadenzas; woodwind arias as bleak as the Last Post; swashbuckling piano contributions that often sound for all the world like a kind of angelic boogie-woogie. His second wife played the *ondes martenot,* a primitive electronic instrument to which he gave a starring role in the *Turangalila Symphony,* perhaps his supreme achievement (*Turangalila,* characteristically, is itself a combination of two Sanskrit words that, combined, mean something like "hymn to love"). Its slithering melodic lines are as beautiful and poisonous as the serpent in Eden. Other indispensable items on any Messiaen shortlist: *Quartet for the End of Time,* written during his confinement in a German prison camp during 1940–41, and his very early miniature *Le Banquet Céleste* for his own instrument, the organ. Now three-quarters of a century old, *Le Banquet* still seems ageless.

zil's amazingly prolific Heitor Villa-Lobos (1887–1959) spent much time there, associating with Milhaud and with the pianist Artur Rubinstein, before returning to his native land. While in France, Villa-Lobos also met fellow expatriate Aaron Copland (1900–90), one of the very first indisputably major composers produced by the United States. (Some would claim this title for Charles Ives [1874–1954], more for his ostensible anticipations of Schoenberg's and Stravinsky's dissonances than through any innate merit; the 1987 findings that Ives deliberately backdated his manuscripts so as to make his own music seem more pathbreaking than it was have done his plausibility no favors.) Copland, after writing in an intensely European—and fairly impenetrable—idiom that struck him as leading to a cul-de-sac, reinvented himself as an Americanist, producing in this new role one critical and popular triumph after another in the orchestral sphere: *Quiet City, El Salón Mexico, Rodeo, Billy the Kid,* and *Appalachian Spring,* to name but five. Other important American composers who emerged between the wars were neo-Romanticist Samuel Barber (1910–81), best known for his *Adagio for Strings,* used on countless funereal occasions in his homeland; and the slightly older Walter Piston (1894–1976), more austere than Copland or Barber and significant above all for his eight symphonies.

※

DESPITE ELGAR'S UNPOPULARITY in old age, the interwar musical conflict between the generations raged less fiercely in England, on the whole, than elsewhere. Vaughan Williams steadily increased his stature, particularly as symphonist, his *Fourth* and *Sixth Symphonies* being as tempestuous as his *Third* and *Fifth* were preponderantly tranquil. Sir Arnold Bax (1883–1953) composed—like his hero Sibelius—seven symphonies, which owed something to Scriabin and Debussy as well as to more recent models. Sir William Walton (1902–83) first achieved worldwide fame with an early aberration, the predominantly witless *Façade*; but he showed his true mettle and steely approach from the 1930s on, with such pieces as his *First Symphony*, concertos for violin, viola, and cello, and the oratorio *Belshazzar's Feast*. Benjamin Britten (1913–76) started at an even younger age than did Walton, and his inherent musicianship was incontestable, however dubious the uses to which he sometimes put it. During the 1930s, Britten joined the "anti-fascist" bandwagon; in 1939, when actually expected to fight against fascism, he responded by fleeing to neutral America. This decision endowed with a certain unintentional comedy his subsequent *War Requiem,* written in serene unawareness of Commando Evelyn Waugh's devastating remark: "If they [artists] want to write about the war, the way is clear for them. They must be, or have been, part of it." Back in England the following decade, Britten wrote several of his finest works: the *Serenade for Tenor, Horn and Strings*; the anthem *Rejoice in the Lamb*; and the opera

Peter Grimes, an artistic (as well as commercial) success that none of his later stage efforts, except perhaps *Billy Budd* and parts of *A Midsummer Night's Dream*, ever matched.

ક

DURING BRITTEN'S YOUTH an unexpected revival of mid- and late-nineteenth-century musical regionalism took place on the Continent. Karol Symanowski (1882–1937), for example—Poland's leading composer since Chopin—showed great partiality toward his country's folk music, and his later works reflect its influence, whereas his earlier works invoke the hothouse atmosphere of Scriabin as well as the orchestral dazzle of Richard Strauss. More systematic in folkloric sympathies were two eminent Hungarians: Béla Bartók (1881–1945) and Zoltán Kodály (1882–1967), who set themselves a task, similar to that of Holst and Vaughan Williams in England, of recording (often with phonographic equipment) as much local folk music as possible before it died out. No mere antiquarians, both Bartók and Kodály believed with proselytizing fervor in the artistic value of what they collected, though they reacted to it very differently. Kodály's best-known compositions are his mostly lighthearted orchestral showpieces (*Dances of Marosszék, Dances of Galanta, Peacock Variations*). Bartók, who had none of Kodály's habitual conviviality, spoke in a musical language much more curt, explosive, and stubborn. His six string quartets are often agonized reminiscences of dance meters blended with snatches of peasant melody to make an utterly individual mixture. In American exile during his last years (as Hungary became more and more pro-Axis), he transcended his New York privations to create perhaps his greatest single piece, the *Concerto for Orchestra*, where the bracing vehemence of his earlier works is combined with a jollity new to him.

⊰⊱

BARTÓK'S ENFORCED DERACINATION indicates that after 1918 it became much harder for composers to avoid overt political issues, although these have been mostly and mercifully absent from this narrative. Between the wars, composers repeatedly needed to wrestle with Big Brother's claims on their allegiance. "We stand for organized terror," thundered Soviet police chief Felix Dzerzhinsky, never one to hide behind euphemism. "Nothing against the state, nothing outside the state," insisted Mussolini, in his case hopefully rather than accurately. "Art will no longer bear experimentation," proclaimed Goebbels. Elizabeth I, Louis XIV, and Napoleon would have considered these sentiments twaddle. After 1918 they were commonplace.

Dmitri Shostakovich (1906–75) incurred the severest injuries from totalitarianism's blowtorch. He woke up one morning, after his First Symphony's première, and found himself nationally famous. Nowadays we find it hard to imagine how novel the Soviet empire seemed in 1926. Could the world's first explicitly godless society endure? Could it produce any art comparable to that produced by those artists misguided enough to have lived under Tsarism? Urgent and portentous questions. Thus, the nineteen-year-old Shostakovich had to be, from the start, music's New Soviet Man. Even if the First Symphony does resemble a collection of Hollywood clichés from before Hollywood clichés were invented, no one denied its composer's talent. Evidently he required pampering. Such pampering's inevitable corollary soon emerged: as the Soviets had raised Shostakovich up, so could they later fling him down. In 1936, they did just that. A *Pravda* editorial denounced his opera *Lady Macbeth of Mtensk*. The Gulag threatened. Shostakovich gave his next (fifth) symphony a groveling subtitle: "An artist's reply to just criticism." The Gulag ceased to threaten. Subsequent effusions included his *Leningrad Symphony*, perhaps the most repetitive exercise in brainless musical demagogy ever perpetrated. Much pseudoscholarship arose after his death to assert that he really hated Soviet communism and furtively derided it via musical codes. Such disingenuous conjecture bespeaks ignorance. Soviet cultural commissars, though thugs, were not fools. Sniffing out satire was part of their job description. If they had even suspected a satirical intention by Shostakovich, he would have been shot—or suffered a fatal car "accident"—before he could say "dialectical materialism."

With Sergei Prokofiev (1891–1953), ambiguity prevailed. Old enough (unlike Shostakovich) to have grown up under the Romanovs, Prokofiev spent most of the years after 1918 in France, Germany, and America. In every respect a greater natural musician than Shostakovich, he excelled especially in his *Third Piano Concerto* and his opera *The Love of Three Oranges*, beautifully crafted, often playful bizarreries. Then, in 1934, he returned to Russia, for reasons he never fully explained. Homesickness played a role. So did vanity: if the Soviets fêted him, who was he to argue? The suspicion grows that the Soviets needed him more than he needed them. Accordingly, they could not stop him from producing—amid some Stalinist junk—great ballets such as *Romeo and Juliet* and *Cinderella*, or from making his cantata *Alexander Nevsky* (originally a movie score) genuinely original.

Italy's Fascisti, for all their tough talk, left musicians largely undisturbed. Ottorino Respighi (1879–1936), the leading Italian composer after Puccini's death, wrote the same types of music that he had always written. A stupendously gifted orchestrator (witness his *Roman Trilogy* symphonic poems), Respighi also had a marked scholarly bent, most likeably evident in his three *Ancient Airs and Dances* suites. Long disparaged as a reactionary hawker of picture-postcards, he benefited during the 1990s from increased CD coverage of his copious and subtle output.

Hitler's Reich forced *its* composers to take sides. The luckier Jewish composers escaped to America: Schoenberg, Zemlinsky (after the *Anschluss*), and Kurt Weill (1900–50), whose brilliantly acrid, derisive, jangling theater music—Prokofiev on steroids—far surpassed its libretti by plagiaristic Marxist ruffian Bertolt Brecht.

Certain other Jewish composers perished in Auschwitz. Webern, for his part, rather welcomed the National Socialists, whom, naïvely, he supposed to be enthusiasts for his work. The National Socialists enlightened him on this important point, and then ignored him. He plugged away at his composition with mole-like diligence until 1945, whereupon an American soldier shot him dead. Avant-garde music had its first bona fide martyr.

Richard Strauss found himself appointed, against his will, to the main NS musical council. He privately reviled his new masters and feared for his Jewish daughter-in-law, whose possible fate concentrated his mind wonderfully. Asked, in an official questionnaire, to name his ancestors (for proof of his Aryan extraction), he cheekily wrote: "Mozart and Wagner." Nazidom alternated between praising and reproving him. Without having to emulate Shostakovich's self-abasement, he survived. So did Carl Orff (1895–1982), of *Carmina Burana* fame. The alleged moral cowardice of Strauss, in particular, should not be sneered at by spoilt Anglo-Saxon pundits whose own political freedom remains untrammeled.

Paul Hindemith (1895–1963), Germany's most intrinsically able post-Strauss composer—he could, incidentally, play almost every orchestral instrument—had been the Weimar Republic's bad boy of music. Wild dissonance, wild blasphemy, jazz elements, parodistic military marches: Hindemith's early output had something to offend everyone. Goebbels called him "atonal" (he was not: indeed, he opposed Schoenberg, as Bartók had done) and, predictably, "degenerate." Other National Socialists thought that Hindemith's populist tendencies made him useful, his Jewish wife notwithstanding. Finally Goebbels won, and Hindemith—who had spent increasing time in Turkey, Westernizing local music education at Atatürk's behest—crossed the Atlantic. His best pieces, more dignified than his youthful indiscretions, include the orchestral works *Mathis der Maler, Nobilissima Visione,* and *Symphonic Metamorphoses on Themes of Weber.*

ক্ষক্ষক্ষ

EPILOGUE:
SINCE 1945

&

THE UPSURGE OF new composing talent that occurred just after World War I failed to reoccur after
World War II. A few young figures did emerge: notably
Gian-Carlo Menotti (1911–2007) and Leonard Bernstein
(1918–90), both eminent in America's musical theater. Yet
most of the newer composers who continued to attract
public attention had first done so before 1945: Britten and
Walton in England; Hindemith in Germany; Messiaen,
Honegger, and Poulenc in France (Milhaud remained
an expatriate); Copland, Barber, and Piston in the U.S.;
Prokofiev and Shostakovich in Soviet Russia. There, in
1948, Cultural Commissar Andrei Zhdanov unleashed
a purge against these two composers and many others, condemning them for "formalism" (never defined)
while insisting that their return to favor (and possibly
their lives) depended on abjectly toeing the government's
line. A similar, albeit less dramatic, process contempo-
raneously began to overtake the Western democracies
and flourished once postwar austerity faded. Throughout these lands—via national broadcasting systems and

other conduits for taxpayers' largesse—Orwellian bureaucrats, answerable to no one, determined the nature of such new music as would gain official sanction. This was no mere charity to occasional deserving cases, such as the Danish and Finnish governments' pensions for, respectively, Nielsen and Sibelius. This was the establishment of veritable states within states. For the first time in Western history outside Axis dictatorships, music would be not something that a private potentate or a church wanted, nor something for which customers had exhibited the faintest enthusiasm, but, rather, something that dragooned audiences would get given, good and hard. Perhaps this bit of social engineering's zenith came, in America, with the establishment of the National Endowment for the Arts, founded in 1965 as part of Lyndon Johnson's much-ballyhooed "Great Society" campaign. Before the war, and especially before the New Deal, most Americans would have found the very idea of the NEA as incomprehensible as—in Charles de Gaulle's caustic phrase—"an Under-Secretaryship of State for Knitting."

Any hopes by such bureaucrats that their beneficiaries would show gratitude were sadly mistaken. A comparatively mild countercultural infantilism characterized Sir Michael Tippett (1905–98), a conscientious objector during World War II and afterwards responsible for numerous operatic portrayals of psychotherapists, freedom fighters, computer mavens, and the occasional Jungian *anima*, "smoking [in Tippett's own words] pipes of peace or pot." Germany's Hans Werner Henze (born 1926) and

Italy's Luigi Nono (1924–90) meant, by contrast, business: both were card-carrying Communists, and Henze devoted part of his oratorio *The Raft of the Medusa* (written in Che Guevara's memory) to proclamations of "Ho, Ho, Ho Chi Minh!" The *Sinfonia* of another Italian, Luciano Berio (1925–2003), guaranteed for itself sycophantic critical coverage by its eulogizing of Martin Luther King Jr. Less political and more giggly in his mischief, America's John Cage (1912–92), when not laboriously wrecking pianos' innards, reached a *reductio ad absurdum* of nihilism in his famous 4'33", which consisted simply of silence for that particular length of time.

Meanwhile, among composers already established, Prokofiev had the misfortune to die on the same day as Stalin. As for Shostakovich, he plumbed new depths of political appeasement, joining the Communist Party for the first time in 1960 and dutifully cosigning official condemnations of dissidents. He thereby attained for himself a paradoxical, spectacular, and, apparently, unshakable reputation for anti-Soviet heroism. It should be noted that, unlike Solzhenitsyn, he had not the faintest capacity for setting an entire alternative value system against Bolshevik terror. Save for some of his string quartets, which may well last, an objective judgment upon most of his music must await a far distant future, when Soviet totalitarians can be discussed as calmly as is Ivan the Terrible.

꧁

Two COUNTRIES SLIGHTLY outside the musical mainstream made notable postwar contributions. Spain produced Joaquín Rodrigo (1901–99), blind from childhood, whose *Concierto de Aranjuez* and *Fantasia Para un
Gentilhombre* are probably the most widely played guitar-
and-orchestra pieces ever written. For a while in the late
1950s and 1960s, Poland became musically fashionable.
Witold Lutosławski (1913–94) managed an odd blend of
surreptitious anticommunism and mildly avant-garde
Western techniques, sometimes suggesting (although
not actually including) improvisation. Krzysztof Penderecki (born 1933) exploded into public consciousness in
1959 with his eardrum-scorching *Threnody for the Victims
of Hiroshima*—a piece thus titled would have found it
harder to fail than to succeed   only to fall from critical
grace with his later, gentler inspirations.

In Germany and France above all, the paucity of
significant new composers was as grim as subsidies were
generous. Karlheinz Stockhausen (born 1928) began his
career with electronic music, continued it with a series—
entitled *Licht*, "Light"—of seven operas, and appeared to
have ended it with a comment describing, or appearing
to describe, the 9/11 terrorist atrocities as "the greatest
artwork ever made." (Afterwards he maintained that his
words had been misinterpreted. We have scant reason to
believe him, given his well-documented threat years be-
forehand to obliterate Vienna: "With one electronic bang,
I'll be able to blow the whole city sky-high!") France's
most eminent living composer is a nonagenarian: Henri

Dutilleux (born 1916), particularly impressive in his chamber music, which somehow refracts Debussy's and Ravel's spirits through a late-twentieth-century prism. Pierre Boulez (born 1925), self-proclaimed "300% Marxist-Leninist," combined a willingness to demand opera houses' destruction with an even greater willingness to demand public funds; his gift for orchestral conducting long ago outstripped his purported creative significance. Far more important than any younger French composer was a Francophile from Japan: Toru Takemitsu (1930–96), who superimposed influences from Debussy and Messiaen on the plangent music of his own people.

Across the Channel, prospects appeared slightly happier. Edmund Rubbra (1901–86) began composing symphonies in the 1930s, but his popularity, such as it was, only really started in the following decade. He thrilled his colleagues by his unaffected yet original style, long-limbed, spacious, possibly the work of an English Bruckner. Sir Malcolm Arnold (1921–2006) wrote numerous celebrated movie scores (and earned an Oscar for one of them, *Bridge on the River Kwai*), though his sometimes effervescent but often grim concert music warrants equal fame. Sir Peter Maxwell Davies (born 1934) trod a somewhat Pendereckian path from ferocious experimentalism (more skittish than Penderecki's) to a sober breadth. A much younger figure to watch is Scotland's James MacMillan (born 1959), who has something of Messiaen's eruptive intensity and spiritual conviction.

DURING THE 1980s there emerged, internationally, an approach loosely called minimalism. Naturally no minimalist composer entirely resembled others, nor would all such composers have accepted the classification of minimalism anyhow. Invariably they modified minimalist techniques to suit their own needs. Still, a family likeness could be detected. Minimalism avoided the wholesale dissonance and rhythmic mush of most twelve-tone music in favor of emphasizing harmonic and melodic essentials, albeit in unpredictable ways: no mere pastiche of earlier manners was involved. Two Americans warrant noting initially. Philip Glass (born 1937) concentrated at first on stage works and film soundtracks but afterwards embarked on symphonies, which sometimes attained real epic merit and were not nearly as repetitive as his earlier compositions had often been. John Coolidge Adams (born 1947) is a more eclectic artist with an improbable (and theatrically effective) penchant for operatic subjects of a grand Handelian type: notably *Nixon in China* and *The Death of Klinghoffer.*

A redoubtable subdivision of minimalism has been called, by some critics, Holy Minimalism: an unexpected return, among composers, not only to musical essentials but also to religion as a fructifying force. Henryk Górecki (born 1933), of Poland, secured brief but exceptional popularity during the early 1990s with his *Symphony of Sorrowful Songs* (actually dating from 1976). Rather more durable in its appeal is the work of Estonia's Arvo Pärt (born 1935). Pärt himself has called his compositional technique "tintinnabuli" (an evocation of bells), but there is more to him than that, notably elements of Gregorian chant, somber pre-Renaissance polyphony, and an atmosphere of dark and menacing forces only distantly perceived. Sir John Tavener (born 1947) had a very indirect route to his eventual fame: originally sponsored by the Beatles' record company, he joined the Russian Orthodox Church in 1977 and thereafter displayed an all-consuming love of Orthodox liturgy, this love both shaping his choral output and spilling over into his instrumental pieces, such as *The Protecting Veil* for cello and orchestra.

❧

THIS EPILOGUE HAS been a mere résumé of post-1945 trends. It could be that the next unambiguously great composer will emerge next week or next year, startling even the keenest-eyed commentators. It could also be that the living composers most praised above will commit some frightful artistic indiscretion that robs them of every claim on posterity's approval. Yogi Berra's words should haunt every music historian: "It is tough to make predictions, especially about the future."

❧❧❧

GLOSSARY

❧

*(for specialized musical items mentioned
in the text that are given in **boldface** type)*

anthem: Originally this word had no connection with national
songs. It referred, instead, to a vocal work for Anglican (Epis-
copalian) church services, often using biblical words, and often
with organ accompaniment. In the *verse anthem,* choral material would be interspersed with passages for soloists, whereas
in the *full anthem* the choir was used throughout. Any list of
leading anthem composers must include Byrd, Purcell, and
Handel.

baroque: A prize instance of how a term of abuse becomes a term
of objective artistic classification ("impressionist" is another
example). Its origin is said to be the Portuguese term *barocco,*
meaning—of all things—an irregularly shaped pearl. Therefore, by analogy, baroque art is irregular, eccentric, lacking the
universal appeal of classical art. Yet today the term *baroque* is
indiscriminately applied to all music written between around
1600 and around 1750, regardless of how deficient in irregular-
ity and eccentricity (indeed how conventional) it may be.

basso continuo: A technique much used in the seventeenth and
eighteenth centuries by which a deep melodic instrument (of-

ten a cello) would take the lowest musical line and, above this, a keyboard or plucked instrument (usually a harpsichord or chamber organ, though sometimes a lute) improvised chordal progressions according to the composer's numeric shorthand, even as it doubled the melodic instrument's material.

bel canto: Literally "beautiful song," but in practice having a much more specific meaning than a mere translation implies. It is always used in connection with the Italian operas of Rossini, Donizetti, and Bellini, and it denotes unfailingly smooth vocalism, with great agility when required, if necessary at the expense of soul-stirring volume.

cantata: This term has several meanings. Secular cantatas, which abounded in the seventeenth and eighteenth centuries, usually consisted of a solo voice with limited accompaniment; they were often designed for domestic use. Sacred cantatas, among which Bach's are preeminent, required a chamber orchestra and frequently several vocal soloists as well as a choir. Bach wrote his for the Lutheran liturgy. Nineteenth- and early twentieth-century composers sometimes used the word to mean any large choral-orchestral piece.

concerto grosso: A concerto which, instead of having merely one or two soloists, has an entire solo ensemble (the *concertino*) vying with the main body of the orchestra (*ripieno*). The plural is *concerti grossi*; Corelli and Handel furnished outstanding instances. Bach's *Brandenburg Concerti* could also be called *concerti grossi*, though Bach did not give them this title. During the late eighteenth century the form died out, but certain twentieth-century composers such as Bohuslav Martinů ("To tell the truth, I am the *concerto grosso* type") revived it.

galant: A French term (literally meaning "gallant") that historians frequently use to describe the late eighteenth century's dominating musical idiom. Less polyphonic than the typical music of the baroque (Q.V.), it tended to consist of melody-plus-accompaniment. It also had a smaller range of harmonies than what went earlier and showed a very much greater reliance upon four-bar phrases. Whereas the word *baroque* is now entirely value-neutral, *galant* often has the implication of shallowness. One would only rarely—and at considerable risk—use *galant* to describe the finest works of Haydn or Mozart, even where they fulfilled the criteria listed above.

libretto: An Italian term for the storyline and words of an opera. So called because in opera's early days these were often supplied for audiences in a "little book."

madrigal: A vital musical genre of the sixteenth and early seventeenth centuries. Mostly secular (though some composers, including Palestrina, wrote sacred madrigals) and frequently amorous, it employed three or more singers. It achieved its greatest popularity in Italy and, later, England. At first it was usually sung unaccompanied, but many of Monteverdi's madrigals have independent instrumental lines, frequently employing a *basso continuo* (Q.V.)

motet: The Catholic equivalent to, and ancestor of, the anthem (Q.V.). Motets were frequently sung during Mass, and often were settings of words that were somehow related to the particular day of the church year. They varied from a few minutes in length to almost half an hour. Palestrina, Lassus, Byrd (for clandestine Catholic devotions), Lully, Rameau, and Bruckner are but a few of the composers who produced motets in bulk.

oratorio: The original Oratory was a group of Catholic priests and laymen founded during the sixteenth century by Saint Philip Neri in Rome. To increase its members' devotion, didactic musical compositions on scriptural subject matter would be commissioned and performed within its ranks, and these compositions, mostly in Latin, came to be called oratorios. Carissimi wrote a great many such works. By Bach's and Handel's time oratorios were usually in vernacular languages and often nonliturgical. Later oratorios of consequence include those by Mendelssohn, Elgar, and Walton.

organum: An early medieval harmonization. At first the organum consisted simply of two voices, one of them singing the main melody (generally plainchant [Q.V.]) while the other sang a countermelody, usually with each note at the same interval from the main melody's. Subsequent instances were more elaborate, and the countermelody developed a good measure of independence.

plainchant: Principal musical manifestation of the Roman Catholic Church from the early Middle Ages till the 1960s' liturgical revolution. It consists of a single melodic line to a Latin text, ideally sung without accompaniment (though sometimes an organ is used to supply harmonies beneath it), and usually moves by stepwise motion or through a few small melodic leaps. Leaps of larger than a fourth, up or down, occur seldom, and generally they illustrate particular words. Most of the local plainchant types that existed before about the eleventh century were discouraged thereafter. The Council of Trent (1545–63) effected further liturgical standardization. Plainchant rhythm's nature remains subject to hot scholarly dispute; most chant performers take a flexible approach to such rhythm, but some liturgists since World War II have argued that chant should be sung to specific meters.

recitative: The nearest that operatic music usually comes to the condition of speech. Normally a recitative propels the narrative along, whereas an aria slows it down and provides an extended comment upon it. Recitative accompanied by only a few instruments is known as recitativo secco (literally "dry recitative"). Orchestrally accompanied recitative, by contrast, is known as recitativo stromentato (literally "instrumented recitative").

symphonic poem, tone poem: Two classifications that emerged in the nineteenth century and mean much the same thing: namely, an orchestral piece that has some program (a nonmusical story, or simply nonmusical subject) determining its structure. (If the subject is nonnarrative, then "tone poem" becomes a more common description.) Notable composers of such works include Liszt, Franck, Smetana, Dvořák, Saint-Saëns, Debussy, Ravel, Borodin, Tchaikovsky, Rachmaninoff, Sibelius, Respighi, and Richard Strauss.

BIBLIOGRAPHY

❧

"A man will turn over half a library to make one book." —Dr. Johnson

FROM THE BEGINNINGS TO 1600

GENERAL HISTORIES: Gustav Reese, *Music in the Middle Ages* (London, 1941); Richard H. Hoppin, *Medieval Music* (New York, 1978); Daniel Leech-Wilkinson, *The Modern Invention of Medieval Music: Scholarship, Ideology, Performance* (Cambridge, 2002); Gustav Reese, *Music in the Renaissance* (New York, 1959); and Allan W. Atlas, *Renaissance Music: Music in Western Europe, 1400–1600* (New York, 1998).

ON CHANT: David Hiley, *Western Plainchant: A Handbook* (Oxford, 1993).

ON THE TROUBADOURS: Simon Grant and Sarah Kay (eds.), *The Troubadours: An Introduction* (Cambridge, 2003).

ON THE *MINNESÄNGER*: Ronald Taylor, *The Art of the Minnesinger: Songs of the Thirteenth Century* (Cardiff, 1968).

ON MACHAUT: Gilbert Reaney, *Guillaume de Machaut* (Oxford, 1971).

ON DUFAY: David Fallows, *Dufay* (London, 1982).

ON JOSQUIN: Richard Sherr (ed.), *The Josquin Companion* (Oxford, 2000).

ON OBRECHT: R. C. Wegman, *Born for the Muses: The Life and Masses of Jacob Obrecht* (Oxford, 1997).

ON LASSUS: Jerome Roche, *Lassus* (Oxford, 1982).

ON PALESTRINA: Jerome Roche, *Palestrina* (Oxford, 1971), and R. J. Stove, *Prince of Music: Palestrina and His World* (Sydney, 1990).

ON GESUALDO: Cecil Gray and Philip Heseltine, *Carlo Gesualdo, Musician and Murderer* (London, 1926).

FROM THE GABRIELIS AND MONTEVERDI TO BACH AND HANDEL

GENERAL HISTORIES: Manfred Bukofzer, *Music in the Baroque Era: From Monteverdi to Bach* (New York, 1947); Claude V. Palisca, *Baroque Music* (Englewood Cliffs, New Jersey, 1990); and John Walter Hill, *Baroque Music* (New York, 2005).

ON THE GABRIELIS: Denis Arnold, *Giovanni Gabrieli and the Music of the Venetian High Renaissance* (Oxford, 1979).

ON SCHÜTZ: Basil Smallman, *Schütz* (Oxford, 2000).

ON MONTEVERDI: Denis Arnold, *Monteverdi* (London, 1963).

ON CAVALLI: Jane Glover, *Cavalli* (London, 1978).

ON LULLY: R. H. F. Scott, *Jean-Baptiste Lully* (London, 1973).

ON COUPERIN: Wilfrid Mellers, *François Couperin and the French Classical Tradition* (London, 1987).

ON RAMEAU: Cuthbert Girdlestone, *Jean-Philippe Rameau: His Life and Work* (London, 1957).

ON PURCELL: Margaret Campbell, *Henry Purcell: Glory of his Age* (London, 1993).

ON HANDEL: Jonathan Keates, *Handel: The Man and His Music* (London, 1985); and Paul Henry Lang, *George Frideric Handel* (London, 1967).

ON CORELLI: Peter Allsop, *Arcangelo Corelli: New Orpheus of Our Times* (Oxford, 1999).

ON VIVALDI: Michael Talbot, *Vivaldi* (London, 1978).

ON ALBINONI: Michael Talbot, *Tomaso Albinoni: The Venetian Composer and His World* (Oxford, 1990).

On Domenico Scarlatti: Ralph Kirkpatrick, *Domenico Scarlatti* (Princeton, NJ, 1983).

On Buxtehude: Kerala J. Snyder, *Dietrich Buxtehude: Organist in Lübeck* (London, 1987).

On Bach: Malcolm Boyd, *Bach* (London, 1983); Christoph Wolff, *Johann Sebastian Bach: The Learned Musician* (New York, 2000); and Klaus Eidam, *The True Life of Johann Sebastian Bach* (New York, 2001).

On Telemann: Richard Petzoldt, *Georg Philipp Telemann* (London, 1974).

From Gluck and Bach's Sons to Beethoven and Schubert

General histories: Philip G. Downs, *Classical Music: The Era of Haydn, Mozart, and Beethoven* (New York, 1992); Julian Rushton: *Classical Music: A Concise History from Gluck to Beethoven* (London, 1986).

On Gluck: Patricia Howard, *Gluck: An Eighteenth-Century Portrait in Letters and Documents* (Oxford, 1995).

On Haydn: Rosemary Hughes, *Haydn* (London, 1962); H. C. Robbins Landon and David Wyn Jones, *Haydn: His Life and Music* (Bloomington, IN, 1988).

On Mozart: Wolfgang Hildesheimer, *Mozart* (New York, 1991); H. C. Robbins Landon, *1791: Mozart's Last Year* (London, 1999); Stanley Sadie, *Mozart: The Early Years* (New York, 2006).

On Beethoven: Barry Cooper, *Beethoven* (Oxford, 2000), and Edmund Morris, *Beethoven: The Universal Composer* (New York, 2005).

On Schubert: Otto Erich Deutsch, *Schubert: A Documentary Biography* (London, 1946), and Brian Newbould, *Schubert: The Music and the Man* (Berkeley, CA, 1999).

From Weber and Rossini to Wagner and Verdi

General histories: Leon Plantinga, *Romantic Music: A History of Musical Style in Nineteenth-Century Europe* (New York, 1984); Charles Rosen, *The Romantic Generation* (New Haven, CT, 1998); Arnold Whittall, *Romantic Music: A Concise History From Schubert to Sibelius* (London, 1987).

On Weber: John H. Warrack, *Carl Maria von Weber* (Cambridge, 1976).

On Berlioz: David Cairns, *Berlioz: The Making of an Artist* (London, 1989), and David Cairns, *Berlioz: Servitude and Greatness* (London, 1999).

On Paganini: Alan Kendall, *Paganini: A Biography* (London, 1982).

On Schumann: Joan Chissell, *Schumann* (London, 1977), and Erik Frederick Jensen, *Schumann* (Oxford, 2001).

On Rossini: Richard Osborne, *Rossini* (London, 1986).

On Donizetti: William Ashbrook, *Donizetti* (London, 1965).

On Bellini: Stelios Galatopoulos, *Bellini: Life, Times, Music,* 1801–1835 (London, 2002).

On Chopin: Arthur Hedley, *Chopin* (London, 1963), and Jim Samson, *Chopin* (Oxford, 1996).

On Mendelssohn: Peter Mercer-Taylor, *The Life of Mendelssohn* (Cambridge, 2000), and R. Larry Todd, *Mendelssohn: A Life in Music* (Oxford, 2003).

On Liszt: Ernest Newman, *The Man Liszt* (London, 1934), and Alan Walker, *Franz Liszt,* 3 vols. (New York, 1983–96).

On Wagner: Ernest Newman, *The Life of Richard Wagner,* 4 vols. (London, 1933–47); Bryan Magee, *Aspects of Wagner* (Oxford, 1988); and Milton E. Brener, *Richard Wagner and the Jews* (Jefferson, LA, 2005).

On Verdi: George Whitney Martin, *Verdi: His Music, Life and Times* (New York, 1983); Mary Jane Phillips-Matz, *Verdi: A Biography* (Oxford, 1993); and John Rosselli; *The Life of Verdi* (Cambridge, 2000).

From Brahms and Bruckner to Sibelius and Stravinsky

ON BRAHMS: Malcolm Macdonald, *Brahms* (London, 1990).

ON BRUCKNER: Derek Watson, *Bruckner* (Oxford, 1996).

ON THE STRAUSS FAMILY: Hans Fantel, *The Waltz Kings* (New York, 1971).

ON GOUNOD: James Harding, *Gounod* (London, 1973).

ON MASSENET: James Harding, *Massenet* (London, 1970).

ON BIZET: Winton Dean, *Bizet* (London, 1975).

ON FRANCK: Laurence Davies, *Cesar Franck and His Circle* (London, 1970).

ON CHAUSSON: Ralph Scott Grover, *Ernest Chausson: The Man and His Music* (London, 1980).

ON SAINT-SAËNS: Brian Rees, *Camille Saint-Saëns: A Life* (London, 1999), and Stephen Studd, *Saint-Saëns: A Critical Biography* (Madison, NJ, 1999).

ON FAURÉ: Jean-Michel Nectoux, *Gabriel Fauré: A Musical Life* (Cambridge, 1991).

ON BALAKIREV: Edward Garden, *Balakirev: A Critical Study of His Life and Music* (New York, 1967).

ON BORODIN: Serge Dianin, *Borodin* (Oxford, 1963).

ON MUSORGSKY: Richard Taruskin, *Musorgsky: Eight Essays and an Epilogue* (Princeton, NJ, 1993).

ON RIMSKY-KORSAKOV: Nikolai Rimsky-Korsakov, *My Musical Life* (New York, 1942).

ON TCHAIKOVSKY: Alexander Poznansky, *Tchaikovsky: The Quest for the Inner Man* (New York, 1991).

ON SMETANA: Brian Large, *Smetana* (London, 1970).

ON DVOŘÁK: John Clapham, *Dvořák* (Devon, UK, 1979).

ON JANÁČEK: Jaroslav Vogel, *Leoš Janáček: A Biography* (London, 1981).

ON GRIEG: John Horton, *Grieg* (London, 1974).

ON NIELSEN: Jack Lawson, *Carl Nielsen* (London, 1997).

ON SIBELIUS: Robert Layton, *Sibelius* (New York, 1993), and Erik Tawaststjerna, *Sibelius*, 3 vols. (London, 1976–97).

On Falla: Burnett James, *Manuel de Falla and the Spanish Musical Renaissance* (London, 1979).

On Sullivan: Michael Angier: *Gilbert and Sullivan: A Dual Biography* (Oxford, 2002).

On Elgar: Jerrold Northrop Moore, *Edward Elgar: A Creative Life* (New York, 1984).

On Delius: Eric Fenby, *Delius As I Knew Him* (London, 1966).

On Holst: Imogen Holst, *Gustav Holst: A Biography* (New York, 1969).

On Vaughan Williams: Wilfrid Mellers, *Vaughan Williams and the Vision of Albion* (London, 1989).

On Mascagni: Roger Flury, *Pietro Mascagni: A Bio-Bibliography* (Westport, CT, 2001).

On Puccini: Mary Jane Phillips-Matz, *Puccini: A Biography* (Boston, 2002).

On Busoni: Antony Beaumont, *Busoni The Composer* (London, 1985).

On Wolf: Frank Walker, *Hugo Wolf: A Biography* (London, 1951).

On Mahler: Donald Mitchell, *Gustav Mahler*, 2 vols. (London, 1995).

On Richard Strauss: Michael Kennedy, *Richard Strauss: Man, Musician, Enigma* (Cambridge, 1999).

On Schoenberg: Walter B. Bailey, *The Arnold Schoenberg Companion* (Westport, CT, 1998).

On Satie: James Harding, *Erik Satie* (London, 1975).

On Debussy: Edward Lockspeiser, *Debussy: His Life and Mind* (London, 1965).

On Ravel: Gerald Larner, *Maurice Ravel* (London, 1996).

On Scriabin: Faubion Bowers, *Scriabin: A Biography of the Russian Composer* (Palo Alto, CA, 1969).

On Rachmaninoff: Max Harrison, *Rachmaninoff: Life, Works, Recordings* (London, 2005).

On Stravinsky: Stephen Walsh, *Stravinsky: A Creative Spring, Russia and France, 1882–1934* (New York, 1999), and Stephen Walsh, *Stravinsky: The Second Exile, France and America, 1934–1971* (New York, 2006).

BETWEEN THE WARS

ON BERG: Mosco Carner, *Alban Berg: The Man and His Work* (New York, 1977).

ON WEBERN: Hans and Rosaleen Moldenhauer, *Anton von Webern: A Chronicle of His Life and Work* (New York, 1978).

ON ENESCU: Noel Malcolm, *George Enescu: His Life and Music* (London, 1990).

ON MARTINŮ: Brian Large, *Martinů* (London, 1975).

ON HONEGGER: Harry Halbreich, *Arthur Honegger* (Portland, OR, 1999).

ON MILHAUD: Paul Collaer, *Darius Milhaud* (San Francisco, 1988).

ON POULENC: Wilfried Mellers, *Francis Poulenc* (Oxford, 1995).

ON MESSIAEN: Christopher Dingle, *The Life of Messiaen* (Cambridge, 2007).

ON VILLA-LOBOS: D. P. Appleby, *Heitor Villa-Lobos: A Life (1887–1959)* (Lanham, MD, 2002).

ON COPLAND: Howard Pollack, *Aaron Copland: The Life and Work of an Uncommon Man* (New York, 1999).

ON BARBER: Barbara Heyman, *Samuel Barber: The Composer and His Music* (New York, 1994).

ON PISTON: Howard Pollack, *Walter Piston* (Ann Arbor, MI, 1982).

ON BAX: Lewis Foreman, *Bax: A Composer and His Times* (Aldershot, UK, 1988).

ON WALTON: Michael Kennedy, *Portrait of Walton* (Oxford, 1989).

ON BRITTEN: Humphrey Carpenter, *Benjamin Britten: A Biography* (London, 1992).

ON BARTÓK: Halsey Stevens, *The Life and Music of Béla Bartók* (New York, 1964).

ON SHOSTAKOVICH: Laurel E. Fay, *Shostakovich: A Life* (Oxford, 2000).

ON PROKOFIEV: Daniel Jaffé, *Prokofiev* (London, 1998).

ON HINDEMITH: Geoffrey Skelton, *Paul Hindemith: The Man Behind The Music* (London, 1975).

EPILOGUE: SINCE 1945

Most of the composers mentioned for the first time in this section are still alive (though not Bernstein, Rubbra, and Takemitsu); therefore biographies of them tend to be defense attorneys' perorations rather than serious judgments. The reader may find something of value in Paul Myers, *Leonrad Bernstein* (London, 1998); Ralph Scott Grover, *The Music of Edmund Rubbra* (Aldershot, UK, 1993); Paul Griffiths, *Peter Maxwell Davies* (London, 1982); Peter Burt, *The Music of Toru Takemitsu* (New York, 2001); Robert Maycock, *Glass: A Portrait* (London, 2002); Thomas May, *The John Adams Reader: Essential Writings on an American Composer* (Pompton Plains, NJ, 2006); and Paul Hillier, *Arvo Pärt* (Oxford, 1997).

Embarking on a Lifelong Pursuit of Knowledge?

Take Advantage of These Resources & Website

The ISI Guides to the Major Disciplines are part of the Intercollegiate Studies Institute's (ISI) Student Self-Reliance Project, an integrated, sequential program of educational supplements designed to guide students in making key decisions that will enable them to acquire an appreciation of the accomplishments of Western civilization.

Developed with fifteen months of detailed advice from college professors and students, these resources provide advice in course selection and guidance in actual coursework. The project elements can be used independently by students to navigate the existing university curriculum in a way that deepens their understanding of our Western intellectual heritage. As indicated below, the Project's integrated components will answer key questions at each stage of a student's education.

What are the strengths and weaknesses of the most selective schools?

Choosing the Right College directs prospective college students to the best and worst that top American colleges have to offer.

What is the essence of a liberal arts education?

A Student's Guide to Liberal Learning introduces students to the vital connection between liberal education and political liberty.

What core courses should every student take?
A Student's Guide to the Core Curriculum instructs students in building their own core curricula, utilizing electives available at virtually every university, and discusses how to identify and overcome contemporary political biases in those courses.

**How can students learn from the
best minds in their major fields of study?**
Student Guides to the Major Disciplines introduce students to overlooked and misrepresented classics, facilitating work within their majors.

Which great modern thinkers are neglected?
The Library of Modern Thinkers introduces students to great minds who have contributed to the literature of the West but are sometimes neglected or denigrated in today's classroom. Figures in this series thus far include Robert Nisbet, Eric Voegelin, Wilhelm Röpke, Ludwig von Mises, and Bertrand de Jouvenel, with many more to come.

Check out www.collegeguide.org for more information and to access unparalleled resources for making the most of your college experience.

ISI is a one-stop resource for serious students of all ages. Visit www.isi.org or call 1-800-526-7022 to add your name to the 50,000-plus ISI membership list of teachers, students, and professors.